Stress Management for Ministers

Stress Management for Ministers

BY

CHARLES L. RASSIEUR

THE WESTMINSTER PRESS
Philadelphia

Copyright © 1982 The Westminster Press

Scripture quotations from the Revised Standard Ver-
sion of the Bible are copyrighted 1946, 1952, © 1971,
1973 by the Division of Christian Education of the
National Council of the Churches of Christ in the
U.S.A., and are used by permission.

BOOK DESIGN BY DOROTHY ALDEN SMITH

First edition

Published by The Westminster Press ®
Philadelphia, Pennsylvania

PRINTED IN THE UNITED STATES OF AMERICA
9 8 7 6 5 4 3 2 1

Library of Congress Cataloging in Publication Data

Rassieur, Charles L., 1938–
　　Stress management for ministers.

　　Includes bibliographical references.
　　1. Clergy—Psychology. 2. Stress (Psychology)
I. Title.
BV4398.R37　　　　253'.2　　　　81–16458
ISBN 0–664–24397–5　　　　AACR2

Dedicated to my many colleagues in ministry who have per-
mitted me the privilege of being their confidant and of walking awhile with them in their journey

Contents

Preface

My purpose in writing this book is to help clergy better manage the stress in their lives so they will increase their effectiveness and their satisfaction in the practice of ministry. My basic thesis is that stress can best be handled when pastors responsibly take care of themselves as persons. In order to offer their best for ministry, I contend that pastors must take more seriously their own selfhood and their own needs. Instead of the denial of self for ministry, I am proposing the recovery of self, with purpose and intention, for the enhancement of ministry!

I bring much personal and professional involvement to this writing project. I am a pastor in The United Presbyterian Church U.S.A., and earlier in my ministry I served three congregations in various pastoral roles. Since that time I have received a Ph.D. degree in pastoral counseling, and my ministry is now that of a specialist. I practice my ministry full time at the North Central Career Development Center in New Brighton, Minnesota, where I work daily with church professionals and candidates for ordination. Since focusing my ministry on pastoral counseling, I have been a supervisor, psychotherapist, and counselor for innumerable clergy and seminarians. In every instance I have viewed these persons as my colleagues in ministry, and I have felt privileged that I could be a resource to them. This book is simply my effort to make a contribution to our common ministry.

An important source of data for this book was tape-recorded research interviews with pastors. Comments by the pastors are included in the following chapters. My purpose in using verbatim observations of clergy is not only to validate the points I develop in each chapter, but more importantly to facilitate a dialogue between the reader and the pastors I have quoted. I am persuaded that the issues I have addressed urgently merit much conversation among clergy. Elsewhere I have claimed that sexuality is the problem that clergymen do not discuss adequately (*The Problem Clergymen Don't Talk About;* Westminster Press, 1976). Here I contend that taking care of one's self has too long been equally taboo for clergy conversation.

I often refer to actual experiences of pastors. However, I have sufficiently altered all details so that no pastor can be identified through the data I have described.

This book is directed to both the practicing pastor and the seminarian who is preparing for ministry. Many will read this book in their own privacy. However, the best way to use it would be for a small group of pastors or seminarians to make it a resource for discussion over at least seven meetings.

Chapter 1 introduces the topic of stress in ministry and discusses symptoms and causes of that stress. Chapter 2 offers a theological rationale for the importance of self-care in a ministry founded upon the pastor's personal wholeness. The next four chapters discuss ten important dimensions of the pastor's life and ministry. In my experience as a counselor to pastors, these ten areas consistently reoccur as areas where clergy either are most vulnerable to stress or have least used resources for coping with stress. Chapter 3 speaks about the personal resources available through the spiritual journey, the pastor's marriage, and one's vocational and leisure interests. Chapter 4 examines the pastor's continuing temptation to be a messiah and the pastor's dilemma about responsibility. Chapter 5 focuses on the tensions involved in the effective use of time and the handling of anger and conflict. Chapter 6 emphasizes the new perspectives gained by pastors for managing stress as they mature through crisis periods of adult growth, seek out the understanding of peers, and make use of institutional resources. Finally, Chapter 7 invites pastors to set goals so they can develop an effective strategy for managing better the stress in their own lives and ministries.

Many persons have helped me with this book, for which I am grateful. I wish especially to express my gratitude to the pastors whose personal testimonies have formed the basis of my research for this book. Their willingness to talk with me in personal terms before a tape recorder has enabled me to include direct quotations that reveal many basic concerns facing all clergy today. I am also indebted to six professional colleagues who have read the full manuscript and made numerous helpful suggestions for its improvement. Each of these six friends has enriched my understanding of ministry: John L. Davis, Nils C. Friberg, Neal E. Lloyd, Betsy L. Nagel, Elizabeth R. Spriggs, and Diane L. Stelter-Tuttle. I must also add my thanks to Edward K. Trefz of Westminster Press for helping me put the manuscript in a more readable style.

Finally, my deepest love and appreciation go to my wife, Ginni, who not only tolerated another writing project with patience and humor but also helped immensely by proofreading the complete manuscript. My sons, Bill and Ted, have also been understanding, and now their father can devote more time to projects nearer their hearts than this book.

In a way it is presumptuous for anyone to write a book about so high a calling as the ordained ministry. Such a book is inadequate, if for no other reason, because of the nature of the topic it presumes to discuss. Nonetheless, I believe the message in this book needs a wide reading and discussion among clergy and seminarians. I am fully responsible for what the reader will find on the following pages, and I will welcome the response of all those who want to probe further the necessities and the challenges of stress management for ministry.

C.L.R.

New Brighton, Minnesota

CHAPTER 1

The Dimensions of Stress in Ministry

The minister of the Christian gospel has responded to a call to one of the most exacting and stressful vocations open to human beings. (Robert D. Phillips and Thomas H. McDill)[1]

Five times I have received at the hands of the Jews the forty lashes less one. Three times I have been beaten with rods; once I was stoned. Three times I have been shipwrecked; a night and a day I have been adrift at sea; on frequent journeys, in danger from rivers, danger from robbers, danger from my own people, danger from Gentiles, danger in the city, danger in the wilderness, danger at sea, danger from false brethren; in toil and hardship, through many a sleepless night, in hunger and thirst, often without food, in cold and exposure. And, apart from other things, there is the daily pressure upon me of my anxiety for all the churches.
(Excerpt from the correspondence of an early pastor)

Stress in pastors wears many faces.

I was caught off guard because there was no warning. Pastor Phil Myers was taking notes as we talked. Nervously he worked the pencil through his fingers and back and forth from one hand to the other. Suddenly he tensed, snapped the pencil in half, and flung both halves of the pencil over my head across the room. In the same motion he leaped to his feet and yelled, "I can't take it any longer!" Again, and louder, "I can't take it!" And again, at the top of his voice, "I can't take it!" The critical pressures in Phil's ministry had reached his breaking point.

13

By contrast, stress in Roger Cotter's life, after more than fifteen years in the ministry, had left him almost like a robot. His movements were slow and mechanical, partly due to the heavy medication his doctor had prescribed to calm his emotions. As he talked he stared blankly straight ahead. He would place his hands carefully behind his head for a few moments, and then restlessly put them in his lap. After he had spoken a few sentences, he methodically lifted his hands and put them behind his head again, repeating this ritual as his voice flatly recited his past disputes with the lay leaders of his congregation.

The many faces of stress have become familiar to me through the years of my ministry. Now I know that when I was a parish pastor I often saw, without recognizing them, signs of stress in the behavior of my colleagues. That was before the term "burnout" was in vogue, when the symptoms of excessive stress within myself and my pastoral colleagues went unnoticed. If my friend Allen—who was always cynical about either his own congregation or the ministry in general—were my neighbor now, I would raise with him the question of the high level of stress he was trying to handle in his life.

Since that time my role as a pastoral counselor and psychologist has forced me to deal with the varied faces of stress in pastors on virtually a day-to-day basis. The symptoms of such stress can claim impressive psychological names. The clinical picture of unmanageable stress frequently includes depression and anxiety. Such symptoms may well also be accompanied by a passive-aggressive style of leadership, or a passive-dependent attitude of hopelessness and despair. Such symptoms confirm that a pastor is already well on the way toward losing the joy and excitement essential for an effective ministry.

Psychological labels alone do not identify all the indicators that a pastor is not adequately coping with the demands of ministry. The breakdown of the pastor's marriage or family life is an altogether too common sign that the proper balance of priorities has been lost. Moderate levels of stress are normal for all families, even those within the parsonage. But too many parsonage families are living in "quiet desperation," trying to hold the lid on deteriorating relationships. The desperation of many such families is related directly to the stress carried by the pastor-family member.

The Anatomy of a Fact of Life

Recently I attended a state convention of psychologists where there were workshops on professional burnout. Listening to psychologists talk about the daily stress they encounter made me feel as if I were listening to a group of pastors. They were saying: "People have such unrealistic expectations of me." "They think I can solve any problem." "Everything is an emergency." "No one understands that I am human, too." "Some days I don't want to see another person!"

Did not those psychologists choose their profession so they could help people in crisis? Now they sound disillusioned and complaining. Did they not know what type of work they wanted when they decided to become psychologists? Perhaps they simply have gone sour on people and for that reason need to get into another line of work.

What happened to those psychologists happens to persons in all the helping professions: they become alarmed because they do not understand their own reactions to stress. Edelwich and Brodsky declare that the recurring effects of such stress, now called burnout, "refer to a progressive loss of idealism, energy, and purpose experienced by people in the helping professions as a result of the conditions of their work."[2] It is a professional problem which "will happen—perhaps repeatedly —in a person's career and must be dealt with on an ongoing basis."[3] The psychologists I was hearing had once thought they were entering a profession that would be continually challenging and fulfilling. It is unquestionably dismaying to any professional person when the accumulated stress of constantly dealing with other people's problems kills the original dedication once felt for helping others.

Hardly anyone would question that stress is a fact of life, particularly if you accept Hans Selye's definition that "stress is essentially the rate of wear and tear in the body."[4] Indeed life is dealing with stress moment by moment. Phillips and McDill have offered their findings on the mental health of Presbyterian ministers and their families in a study completed for the Presbyterian Church U.S. The authors distinguish between stress and the tension which is the body's response to the stress.

> *Stress* may be defined as the summation of all those stimuli (physical, intellectual, interpersonal and intrapsychic) which demand attention and assimilation at any given moment. Regardless of the source or mode of the stimulus, the human organism enters a state of tension upon receiving any stimulus. The state of tension is relieved when (and only when) the physical stimulus is "handled" by acceptance, resolution, or reconciliation. Optimally the human organism remains sufficiently attuned to incoming stimuli to provide zest, sufficiently frustrated by contingency to provide challenge, meaning and purpose, and sufficiently gratified in achieving needs and goals to provide a reservoir of physical, intellectual, and emotional energy.[5]

Even as I sit here typing I must deal with stress and the resulting tension that I am experiencing. Intrapsychic stress prods me to type ten pages of material today. The physiological stress in my body suggests it would be more enjoyable to play basketball than to sit on this uncomfortable chair for hours at a time. There are also the mechanical and intellectual stresses of manipulating a machine to put sentences expressing coherent thoughts on a sheet of paper.

Selye has taken a slightly different approach to the definition of stress. Instead of regarding stress as the demand made on the organism, as Phillips and McDill suggest, Selye proposes that stress be regarded as the response the body makes to any demand upon it. He distinguishes "eustress" (good stress: e.g., joy, fulfillment, satisfaction) from "distress" (excessive levels of damaging stress).[6]

Thus "stress" may appropriately refer either to the source of demands made upon us or to the response we make to those demands. Throughout this book, "stress" will be used to refer to both demands and responses. The context of the discussion should make clear how the term is being used.

The Professional Burnout Syndrome

Stress, the tension it produces, and the responses we make to it, is broadly what living is about. Selye concludes: "The goal is certainly not to avoid stress. Stress is part of life."[7] More recently, professionals within the ministry and related helping professions have been much concerned about "burnout." Herbert J. Freudenberger was one of the first to define and explain the dynamics of burnout among professional persons. Freudenberger refers to the dictionary, which defines "to burn out" as "to fail, wear out, or become exhausted by making excessive demands on energy, strength, or resources."[8] He and his colleagues were seeing just that type of exhaustion among their staff members who had, for whatever reasons, become increasingly ineffective in fulfilling their professional responsibilities.

According to *The World Book Dictionary*, "burned out" applies to the apathetic, exhausted individual. The same dictionary explains the aerospace applications of the word "burnout" and "burnout velocity."[9] In the flight of a rocket, "burnout" refers to the extinguishing of the flame in a rocket engine when fuel is exhausted or shut off according to plan. The burnout velocity is the speed at which the rocket is going at the instant of burnout. There is a corresponding burnout velocity at which many professional persons continue to move after they exhaust their own personal resources and can no longer function effectively.

LeRoy Spaniol, assistant professor of rehabilitation counseling at Boston University, observes: "There are many ways to define burnout, but basically it means feeling locked into a job routine. Burnout disproportionately strikes those in the helping professions—teachers, counselors, social workers."[10] Spaniol speaks of first-, second-, and third-degree levels of burnout. First-degree burnout is mild, characterized by short-lived bouts of irritability, fatigue, and frustration. Second-degree burnout is more serious because the symptoms in first-degree burnout begin to last two weeks or more. The more severe third-degree burnout is indicated by physical ailments such as ulcers, chronic back pain, and migraine headaches.[11]

Edelwich and Brodsky have identified four states that lead to burnout or disillusionment among persons in the helping professions. *Enthusiasm* marks the first stage of high hopes, high energy, and unrealistic expectations when one is new to the job and has yet to find out what the job really entails. The next stage is characterized by *stagnation* because now the job is not thrilling enough to replace everything else in life. The third stage is filled with *frustration* because one questions the job itself and the value of the work one is trying to accomplish. Chronic frustration leads to the fourth stage of *apathy*, when one tries to meet only the minimum requirements.[12]

Five members of the Department of Psychiatry at the University of Texas Medical School in Houston have described their findings regarding the diminished functioning of medical personnel, corporate executives, lawyers, researchers, and individuals later diagnosed as alcohol or drug abusers. This professional burnout syndrome is identified by a person's decreased efficiency, initiative, interest in work, and performance level. Other related symptoms include:

(1) feelings of exhaustion and fatigue and a sensation of being physically run down
(2) frequent headaches and gastrointestinal disturbances, which may be accompanied by:
(3) weight loss
(4) sleeplessness
(5) depression
(6) shortness of breath

Specific behavioral changes may include the following symptoms:

(1) lability or instability of mood
(2) blunting or flattening of affect and emotional responses
(3) quickness to anger, with increased irritability
(4) diminished frustration tolerance
(5) suspiciousness, which at times may create unrealistic fears and concerns
(6) feelings of helplessness
(7) increased levels of risk-taking

These physical and behavioral symptoms may also be accompanied by increased chemical use and dependency. Persons in the advanced stages of burnout may turn to and make excessive use of tranquilizers, barbiturates, narcotics, and alcohol, which may lead to addiction.[13]

Major Areas of Stress in Ministry

The areas of stress and burnout reported by secular professional persons are quite similar to the areas of stress experienced daily by pastors. The question is not how to rid ministry of stress. The issue is how to keep it at a manageable level so that a pastor does not conclude that the only viable option is to exit the ministry.[14] There is much evidence that clergy as a group are finding ways to cope with the threat of burnout. Large numbers are not leaving the parish ministry because of the pressures in the local church. In 1969 Seward Hiltner surveyed the reports that clergy could not handle the stress of the local parish, and he concluded that pastors were dealing with stress better than most professional persons. He declared:

> There are times when I wish more ministers were breaking down—with heart disease, [high] blood pressure, cancer, psychoses, or criminal impulses. If they did, it might show that they were unhappy victims of commitment to their difficult and complex jobs. The fact is, however, that ministers are the most long-lived of all professional men, and their incidence of serious mental illness is low.[15]

Hiltner's observation was confirmed by the reports of approximately twelve thousand Protestant pastors who, despite recurring periods of career-related stress, claimed to have reached a satisfactory resolution of their problems, often with a satisfying sense of personal growth through the experience of stress.[16]

Few pastors are overwhelmed by the pressures of ministry, and even fewer are leaving the professional ministry. Still, many pastors feel that the sacrifices they must make for their calling are unnecessary and the demands upon their families have little to do with furthering God's Kingdom. The question before the church is how to help its professional ministers cope more effectively with stress so they not only serve others with greater joy but also find genuine personal renewal through their calling. When ministry fails to generate a spirit of renewal within the minister, then this question must be asked: Is the pastor overtaxed with too much stress? The possibility that many pastors have lost the joy of giving and renewal makes the whole question of stress management for ministry a critical question for the church in the 1980s.

It is important for pastors to be aware of the areas where they are vulnerable to stress. To be forewarned can help a pastor to monitor the level of pressure felt in the more stressful areas of ministry. The pastor who is unaware of the potential pitfalls is less likely to cope effectively when stressful situations are encountered. There is overall agreement among those who work with pastors as to what the principal areas of stress are in the parish ministry. Different writers may use differing labels, but the picture that emerges is remarkably similar from writer to writer.

Donald Houts of the United Methodist Church reports from two different sources regarding the characteristic problems of those in the pastoral ministry. The first came from district superintendents in one United Methodist annual conference. They consistently reported the following five areas of concern expressed by the pastors in the conference:

(a) loneliness; (b) conflicts regarding expectations placed upon spouses (especially with regard to employment and church attendance and involvement); *(c)* feelings of inadequacy; *(d)* intellectual and spiritual malaise; and *(e)* lost sense of meaning regarding their work. The latter two were particularly characteristic of those who had served in ministry for longer periods of time. As one very "successful" pastor of a large, prestigious church reported: "After twenty-three years of it, I'm not honestly sure my work has made any difference at all."[17]

The other source described by Houts tells of the five most representative problems of those pastors who have sought help at the Menninger Foundation.

1. Overextension—the feeling of having too many commitments that vied for time and energy.
2. Imprecise competence—the feeling that they functioned primarily "by the seat of their pants," without being sure of why they did what they did.
3. Inadequate resources—the feeling that there was no adequate "backup system," . . . and that they had to be satisfied with leftover resources of time, talent, and substance.
4. A desperate groping for relevant religious faith. Pastors themselves are subject to so many demands from others that they begin to feel in need of a pastor themselves. Many experienced this as a gradual sense of losing the reality of the faith that they proclaimed, . . . playing their roles with decreasing involvement, commitment, and integrity.
5. Lack of accomplishment. How does one measure the impact of preaching? How does one measure the impact of a midnight crisis in the home of a parishioner? How does one measure one's influence in a summer camp program over a period of years? While gratification is important to continued productive work, it is difficult to measure the intangible rewards and accomplishments that are so basic in the ministry.[18]

Lloyd Rediger, an experienced counselor of pastors, offers an observation about the major source of stress for clergy. He thinks that the pastor's personal and professional identities, and the pastor's religious faith, are all combined in the single pastoral role, thus causing a continuing identity crisis for the minister.[19] Margaretta Bowers has remarked on the profound disappointment pastors feel who enter ministry out of their need to find love; she also notes the pressures felt by clergy because of the sharp contrast between their professional image and their humanity.[20] The stress of the pastor's identity crisis was recognized by Urban Holmes as occurring in the disparity between the congregation's expectations of a pastor and the biblical model for ministry: "It is remarkable how many a clergyman fulfills the *congregation's* image of the pastor, which is utterly incongruent with the Gospel's."[21] Donald Smith's study helped to clarify the stress created for pastors by role conflict and role ambiguity.[22] And the authors of the report on *Stress in the Ministry* concurred with other researchers in finding that the roots of work-related stress include conflicting role expectations, inadequate support systems, institutional rigidity in the face of major change, ideological conflict, personal and family deprivations, and the very nature of the ministry itself.[23]

From my own perspective, five salient areas of stress for clergy especially need to be understood today.

1. *The ordination contract.* In many respects the ordination of a minister resembles a marriage and reflects some of the struggles common to many marriages. With the solemn exchange of vows, the laying on of hands, and the saying of prayers, the church and a minister enter into an intimate, lifelong covenant relationship. Just like a marriage, the relationship will profoundly affect both parties; neither will ever be the same again. Ordination is an act of marriage that follows, in most denominations, a protracted courtship. During that time both parties have examined each other's history, strengths, and

limitations with as much objectivity as is possible during courtship. Then promises of mutual commitment and faithfulness are made.

We know that with each verbal marriage contract there is also a more detailed unspoken contract. Because it is unspoken, the various clauses do not ordinarily become known to both parties until years later when severe conflict erupts.[24] Hardly any couple escapes the conflicts that arise from such nonverbal contracts. The unspoken clauses often involve such questions as: Who makes final decisions about spending family money? Who stays home to care for the children? Who goes out into the world to seek a career? Because both partners usually have so much at stake around their unspoken expectations, marriage counselors know that the renegotiation of the nonverbal marital contract is essential to most marriage counseling.

Just as in every marriage an unspoken contract is open to misunderstanding, so too the unspoken ordination contract between pastor and church can easily be misunderstood. Let us consider what the typical candidate for ordination brings to ministry and to the ordination contract.

Leadership potential is evident in most persons preparing for the ministry. Even if such persons are shy or introverted, they have had numerous fieldwork experiences and training in seminary to give them adequate skills in working with both small and large groups of people. Most students have received quite positive affirmation because of the leadership qualities their friends and colleagues have recognized in them as they have matured in the church.

Besides having good leadership skills, the candidate is usually more idealistic than the average person. This capacity for idealism enables the candidate to respond to the gospel and be excited by a vision of what might be accomplished through ministry. With such idealism goes a high level of dedication to pay the high price that the gospel requires for faithful ministry.

In addition to these attributes, most seminarians are also sensitive and responsive to human need. They feel they should be involved and contributing to the solution of critical problems facing the church. Most other people would choose not to be so involved.

Somehow related to this response is the candidate's need for continuing affirmation. Most likely, since the day the candidate first breathed the word that ministry would be his or her career goal, subtle and obvious praise have created an unnatural environment around the candidate. The candidate has been not only set apart but set upon a pedestal.[25] Some days being on the pedestal feels good; but the dread of falling from the pedestal is also present. And thus is born the fear of rejection that haunts so many pastors.

The church's part of the ordination contract is, first of all, to offer unlimited needs, both human and organizational, to challenge the new pastor's dedication. Because it is the inherent nature of the gospel to address every human condition, the church promises the new pastor a job that can never be completed. The work can never be finished despite the modern marvels of committee meetings and copying machines!

Secondly, it is the nature of the church that affirmation and praise are usually given only when high expectations have been satisfied. Simply preaching a sermon is an act that in itself merits praise, but it must be a remarkable sermon before the pastor receives much positive affirmation. And even though the pastor has had an extraordinary week of emergencies expertly handled, there is always something someone can find to criticize. Pastor Ruth Dawson explained this dilemma for pastors in these words:

Because they do not know what your schedule has been and what you've accomplished, they usually put on you what there is left to be done. They are only aware of what has not been done. And if you have indeed seen Mrs. Smith that week, they are not terribly pleased or impressed, because you really should have seen her three weeks ago, and you still have not seen Mrs. Jones, have you!

The observation is correct that "ministry is like no other profession. . . . People feel free both to admire [ministers] extravagantly and criticize them severely."[26]

The unspoken dimensions of the ordination contract leave much room for misunderstanding and stress between the pastor and the parishioners. At its worst, ministry can degenerate into the frustrated exercises of a high-achiever who is afraid of rejection, responding anxiously to vague and limitless expressions of need. The pastor assumes that a little more effort will bring the hoped-for praise. In the meantime, the laity have little idea how much impact their casual criticism has upon their pastor. While there is no precise way to rate ministerial effectiveness, it is easy for laypersons to suspect that the pastor is wasting time during the week and showing up only for Sunday mornings. What is both sad and amazing is that such misunderstandings and bitter feelings can arise from the most mature and responsible pastors and lay church leaders alike.

2. *The ten-year sprint.* Despite all appearances to the contrary, most clergy are quite competitive. In this respect, clergy are like their colleagues in other professions. At the benediction concluding their seminary commencement exercises, the gun goes off for the race to see who will be at the head of the pack ten years later.[27] Clergy do not talk openly about all the facts of life, but they know them very well. There are few desirable churches—those offering the most desirable sala-

ries. Many pastors are called to serve, but only a handful are selected for the prominent pulpits or appointed to positions of power. The way to the top for many pastors, despite what the New Testament may say, is to work hard and gain the attention of the right people.

Ambition can be a positive virtue, especially if it motivates creativity and dedication. However, the ministerial ten-year sprint with its pressure to work sixty to eighty hours a week comes when many pastors are beginning a marriage and a family. The pastor's spouse and children require more time and support during this period than at any other time in the life of the family. So it comes as no surprise if at some point within the first ten years the pastor is overwhelmed with exhaustion, disillusionment, and the protests of an angry spouse. The reports of over thirty-five hundred pastors confirm that stress is most likely to occur in the early years of ministry.[28] It is during the first ten years of ministry that many pastors wistfully ask themselves, "Is this why I entered the ministry? Is it really worth it?"

Some young pastors put in the long hours simply because of the idealism and dedication that are characteristic of most persons entering the ministry. A fellow pastor once confided to me that when he was courting his wife he honestly told her that if they married, she needed to understand that for him his ministry would have a higher priority in his life than his marriage and family. After more than ten years, he was still maintaining that order of priorities, and he had finally received a call to a prestigious church. At least he had told his wife from the outset what was ahead of her.

3. *Unique stresses for female clergy.* Women are entering the professional ministry in greater numbers. Despite the controversies about ordaining women, increasingly women are seeking ordination as the fulfillment of their deep calling to service. As women are graduating from

seminary they are finding a wider acceptance, in many denominations, in staff positions in larger congregations or solo pastorates in smaller, rural congregations. The real test for the church, however, comes when these female pastors are ready to make their second move and desire consideration as the solo pastor or the senior pastor of the larger, more influential congregations.

The women entering the ministry are ready to compete on an equal basis with their male colleagues, and they want to be recognized as full partners in ministry. However, male clergy have much reassessing to do in their feelings and attitudes before they will be fully ready for women to be total partners in the ordained ministry. Subtly it is communicated to female clergy that they should remember who they are and what their place is. One male pastor tried to dismiss Pastor Mary Gamer in a committee meeting when she challenged his point of view. The clergyman actually said, "I am old enough to be your father, so I know that my opinion has more experience behind it." Mary Gamer's response was to remind the clergyman that she knew he was only forty-six and that she was forty-two! Too often female clergy hear the message that they are little girls trying to play at a man's game.

An additional issue for women in the ministry is the stress of being the token woman. One female pastor, after only two years in the ministry, was asked to join one of the most influential church committees in her region. She felt ambivalent about adding this further responsibility to her workload.

> If I say yes, I am saying, "Yes, it is O.K. for you to appease your need and put me on there." And if I say no, I am keeping every other woman off for the next eight years because they will keep telling everybody, "We asked one and she said no."

Pastor Gail Snyder has observed that women in the ministry face other critical problems as well. The divorced female pastor who is a parent hears from the parishioners, "How can we accept your ministry when you 'abandon' your children to come to our evening meetings?" But the single-parent male pastor is applauded for his bravery in trying to mix parenting and ministry.

Snyder also raises the concerns of the single female pastor who is sent two conflicting messages. On the one hand, it is implied that she should not be socially active, seeking social opportunities to be with males. But on the other hand, she is supposedly inadequate because she does not have a married relationship with a male. If she has children, people expect her to stay at home with her children, and through her children to meet her needs for intimacy and sharing. This viewpoint, says Snyder, assumes "that sexual intimacy is not necessary for women." Snyder adds, "If female clergy do not find sufficient opportunities for intimacy outside the congregation, they are vulnerable to becoming workaholics because of their need for socialization through the congregation."

Even apart from their needs for intimacy, female clergy have the issue of how to relate with their male colleagues. One female pastor declared her frustration that even though she and several male pastors were going to the same meeting in another community, none would even call her to ask if she would care to share a ride. It was always left up to her to ask for a ride.

Pastor Snyder spoke from her own experience when she said that the greatest opposition to female clergy often comes from other women in the congregation!

By and large the most inflexible opposition to the professional woman pastor comes from women in mid-life who,

while denying strenuously the sexist basis of their com-
plaint, question the adequacy of the female to pastor
since she cannot therefore devote one hundred percent of
her energy to motherhood and because they cannot listen
to a soprano voice in the pulpit. One of the complaints I
have received from such women is that my earrings are
distracting!

Another problem for many a woman in ministry is
that she was reared to assume that it is her primary
responsibility to be sure the home operates smoothly.
Then when she enters ministry, the female pastor often
carries that old expectation with her, so she ends up
feeling that she has two highly demanding professions:
ministry and home management! That common role
conflict requires both the woman and her husband to
examine their expectations of each other so she does noí
unfairly carry a heavier burden, one that social custom
has placed on her.

Female clergy will greatly enrich the church's ministry, as indeed they already have in a wide range of areas.
However, women who have chosen to enter the professional ministry must cope with added stress in many
respects simply because they are women.

4. *Clergy couples.* When husband and wife are both
ordained, a new type of stress is encountered by both the
couple and the church. Though the number of such couples is increasing at a surprising rate, the church at the
judicatory level and the parish level is still learning how
to accept and work with clergy couples.[29] In the fall of
1978, at the Ecumenical Clergy Couple Consultation, it
was estimated that there were as many as 5,750 clergy
couples in all branches of Protestantism in the United
States. Moreover, if the current rate of increase continues, by 1984 the total number will double within main-
line Protestant denominations![30]

One of the main problems faced by such a couple is

to find a call or an appointment, either to a joint ministry in the same congregation or to settings in close proximity to each other. Many combinations of ministry have been put together by such couples. One partner may serve in an institutional chaplaincy while the other serves a congregation. Both may serve in a yoked parish, or both may serve the same church.

Apart from the normal stresses of any dual-career marriage, clergy couples must usually deal with two additional sources of stress. One involves the couple's marital relationship, as they must constantly clarify their individuality. Unless both persons are serving in geographically separated settings, their parishioners will naturally assume that they are a single unit. Everyone comes to believe that messages for Tom can very easily be given to Susan, and vice versa. Does it not make sense to expect that such a devoted couple eats, breathes, and sleeps the church when they are alone together in their home? Certainly Susan knows as much about the women's association as Tom does, and Tom should naturally take Susan's place when she cannot attend a trustees meeting.

Wrong! Clergy couples must work hard to preserve their individuality and not to become confused themselves. When a couple begin to get trapped in their parishioners' perception that they are Siamese twins, their marital relationship is usually put under much greater tension because they have begun to lose the important sense of their own individuality, their uniqueness as persons.

A second and related problem arises because each person will have different areas of strength and skill as well as different professional limitations. This can lead to competition and unfavorable comparisons both by their parishioners and by judicatory leaders. Susan may well be a more dynamic preacher and a better administrator, while Tom's strength may be in pastoral care and youth work. Unless a couple can learn to be comfortable with their natural differences and unless parishioners appreciate the unique contributions each spouse has to offer, far too much stress will be placed on the couple, their marriage, and their ministries.

These and other difficult issues add to the unique sources of stress when both husband and wife are ordained. The church has much more to learn about the needs of clergy couples so that excessive stress will not prevent them from making their contribution as professionals in ministry.

5. *Who is sick?* Not long ago I was talking with an experienced pastor about stress in his life and ministry. The conversation ranged over a number of issues including how this pastor dealt with anger, handled his relationships in his family, and managed his earlier need to be a messiah who was busy doing good all the time. As we finished our conversation, I asked him how he perceived the leadership of his denomination, particularly at the state level, and their attitudes toward the concerns he was expressing about ministry and the management of stress. He replied:

> I sense that the leadership of the church is becoming more aware of a need to address itself to these issues but has not done it. But I don't think that the leaders of the church have dealt with these issues in their own lives, and therefore find it very difficult to deal with them as leaders in the life of congregations and pastors. They superficially react only when a parish pastor finds herself or himself in trouble. Then they make a judgment that something is wrong with the pastor and send the pastor for career development counseling. And if the pastor is "wacko" they send her or him out of the state.

As a group, church administrators at judicatory levels are troubled by the concerns of their pastors. However, that caring is unevenly perceived by the clergy in the parish. Most often pastors feel that evidences of stress will be taken by others to mean that they are weak, incompetent, or sick.

Occasionally a pastor is incompetent. But it is rarely acknowledged that the pastor is a human being whose professional functioning has been greatly shaped by the system within which he or she serves. The health of the church will be reflected in the health of its pastors. The church at every level will make greater strides in relieving the stress from various sources felt by clergy when it fully acknowledges that the church as an institutional system is the primary context for the stress affecting pastors.[31] So the issue of stress is a concern that involves everyone in the church at every level, not just the pastor who is expressing the pain through various symptoms. Excessive stress in pastors' lives and in their ministries is a problem that calls for the church's own self-examination at all levels of ecclesiastical life.

The Coping Pastor

Not long ago I had lunch with an old friend. We had not seen each other since serving churches in the same city nearly ten years previously. I left that city three years before he did. We were both much surprised that after several moves we ended up working near each other again.

I was struck by my friend's continuing gentle, easy smile and the excitement for ministry still reflected in his eyes. When I had known him before, he was serving a racially integrated church in a neighborhood that had rapidly changed. He knew what it meant to be an authentic mediator to two different cultures, earning the trust and admiration of both. Though much at home with his white parishioners in their comfortable homes miles from the church, he was probably more at home playing in the streets around the church with shouting and laughing black children. And always there was the calmness, the genuineness, the wisdom—and the steady smile and the glowing eyes. My friend was re-created by ministry. He did not just survive the loss of members, the neighborhood political battles, the break-ins at the church, the vandalism. My friend periodically "reenlisted" in ministry because it was too exciting and too much fun to think of doing anything else.

The list of stress factors in ministry is a serious matter that merits the study of all who make decisions at every level of the church. Despite the promised difficulties inherent in any ministry, many pastors are not only surviving but are doing so with genuine satisfaction in their work. Seward Hiltner is right: most clergy are not breaking down or falling apart under the pressures. Although many pastors show evidence of an overburdening level of stress upon themselves and their families, most refuse to leave the professional ministry for another vocation.

My friend with the gentle smile belongs to a breed of pastor set apart. He belongs among those pastors who are not just getting by, but who, some days at least, would even admit to loving the ministry for what it has done for them. The other quality I have noticed about such pastors is that they like to be around people, and others really like to be around them. There is a buoyant spirit about such pastors. They are free from underlying cynicism, depression, or sarcasm that can leave you with the impression that something is eating at a pastor's insides. On the contrary, such pastors have a sense of being present in an uncomplicated manner as they meet parishioners and colleagues at any level of life. People are drawn to these pastors in a comfortable way because there is a love within them that contagiously enlivens the spirits of those they meet. Despite the stress, pastors like my friend joyously thrive on ministry.

How do we account for pastors like these, who thrive despite the obvious stresses of ministry? What explains their enthusiasm for ministry? Is it the result of extraordinary commitment and spiritual dedication? Has God favored them more than others? Are they more religious, or perhaps wiser, or just tougher-skinned? Certainly it is not that they make more money, or that they do not serve difficult pastorates. Some are serving congregations others would not care to serve. Indeed, if the church could discover what motivates such pastors maybe there could be important lessons to be learned for all who are in the ministry.

From my own observations, after working with many clergy and seminarians, I have discovered a consistent characteristic among those who find so much satisfaction in ministry. This singular characteristic can take on varying dimensions and manifest itself in a variety of ministry styles, but the essential characteristic is a strong, firm sense of self and personal identity.

These pastors are not egotists with the type of bravado that thinly veils inner insecurity. No, they have clear boundaries around their own selfhood. Their grasp on their own self-identity is so firm that they may often appear to be overconfident. It is characteristic of such pastors that they bite off more than they can chew, but it does not choke them. Another way to put it is that they are risk takers, particularly in their relationships with other persons. They risk being close, they risk being loving, and they risk telling the truth. Of course they know what it means to be afraid, but they have learned somewhere that there is a promise of new life implicit in every risk, no matter what the odds against them. They will listen to Paul's recounting of his adventures in ministry and respond, "Why not?" They are ready because they know who they are. Whether or not they have ever given it explicit thought does not matter; their confidence and their ability for handling stress are rooted in their positive regard for themselves.

Rarely has high positive regard for one's self been discussed as an essential factor for faithful and effective ministry. If it is true that pastors who distinguish themselves by their enjoyment of ministry have in common a high regard for their own needs and self-identity, then the church needs to reassess the traditions and the misunderstandings that have made it taboo for the clergy to acknowledge openly that they do hold their own selves in high esteem. Perhaps having a positive regard for one's self does not sound spiritual or religious. It has the sound of selfishness, egotism, or self-centeredness, and none of these has ever been looked upon as a positive attribute for a Christian minister.

But there is too much evidence now for the church to ignore. Ministry that joyfully copes with stress is grounded in centered self-identity. The recovery of self is the essential prerequisite for all ministry.

CHAPTER 2

Recovering Self for Ministry

> A self is not a thing that may or may not exist; it is an original phenomenon which logically precedes all questions of existence. . . . Man is a fully developed and completely centered self. (Paul Tillich)[1]

> If we cannot say yes to ourselves we cannot offer ourselves unselfishly to anyone else; we can surrender to them, but we will have lost the gift that we were asked to bring. (David B. Harned)[2]

All pastors hear words similar to the following when they are ordained and whenever they are installed in a new pastorate:

> Whoever among you wants to be great must become the servant of all, and if he wants to be first among you, he must be the slave of all men! Just as the Son of Man came not to be served, but to serve, and to give his life to set others free.[3]

The ordination or installation service may well include the reading of Phil. 2:1–11, which declares that Christ Jesus "emptied himself, taking the form of a servant," and advises: "Do nothing from selfishness or conceit, but in humility count others better than yourselves."

Pastor Paul Michalson is familiar with those words. His parents were missionaries, so he was reared in a family dedicated to ministry. He is now highly respected as the pastor of a downtown congregation in a major metropolitan area. His understanding of Christian servanthood, particularly for pastors, is rather blunt and to the point.

> We are servants of Christ, we are servants of the Word. Certainly in our life, in our ministry we should model that. But that does not mean that we have to be someone's flunky. A lot of ministers that I observe tend to be the church's flunky. They'll do everything. And they do that in the name of being a servant. But I would just question how effective they are in what they are trained and called to do, and secondly, whether that is the most effective form of servanthood.

The Model for the Church's Ministry

All ministry is defined and measured by the ministry of Jesus Christ. All who respond to his call to live a life of faithfulness to God are called to a life of giving themselves for others. The importance of this essential point was emphasized by Goodykoontz in his study of the Reformed tradition: "The minister is one who serves. In Jesus we see the nature of the gospel ministry. . . . Jesus was a servant."[4] The Suffering Servant of the fifty-third chapter of Isaiah is a theme for Jesus' ministry that runs as a common thread through the Gospel accounts. Indeed, the stark contrast between Jesus' conception of ministry and the disciples' notion of greatness is vividly portrayed in Luke 22:24–27. In that account, the disciples fell into argument about their position, rank, and power. Jesus turned the tables on them by his words: "I am among you as one who serves" (v. 27).

There is no way properly to view ministry in any other context. The power of the Christian ministry is rooted in the paradox of Jesus' ministry. He who could have claimed unspeakable power died powerless, and in so doing he accomplished what could not be done any other way, the redemption of the world for God's purpose. As James Smart has observed: "Strangely, it was in [Jesus'] dying that his ministry was fulfilled with the profoundest power."[5] Of this paradox Daniel Jenkins declared: "The whole office of the ministry is to be understood as the expression in the Church of this fundamental paradox—that Jesus Christ, the Son of God, the King of all the earth, comes and establishes His kingly rule among men in the form, not of a king, but of a servant."[6]

The evidence is clear. The power of Jesus' ministry was rooted in God's love taking a form that is a stumbling block to human sensibilities. The servant, despised and rejected, is the means God uses to overcome the profound blindness and stubbornness of the human heart. Humility is the mark of any ministry that would be part of God's continuing redemptive work in the world. It matters not where one serves in the church.

> The Greek word for "ministry" is *diakonia*. . . . Thus also, even today, if we wish a term which includes the archbishop as well as the pastor of the humblest congregation, we speak of "the ministry." And so, in word at least, we obey Jesus' injunction: "Whoever would be great among you must be your servant [*diakonos*], and whoever would be first among you must be slave of all" (Mark 10:43–44).[7]

To be a servant clearly calls for one to deny one's self. The function of a servant is to be in subjection and compliance. Indeed, the self, with its desires, urges, and impulses, is generally viewed as the chief impediment to the complete Christian life and service. The importance of freedom from self is expressed in the words of hymns commonly sung by Christians:

> Amazing grace!
> How sweet the sound
> That saved a wretch like me![8]

Holy Spirit, love divine,
Glow within this heart of mine;
Kindle every high desire;
Perish self in your pure fire.[9]

The denial of one's self, the setting aside of one's interests, needs, and desires has become the highest goal for ministry. This is the demand that Jesus makes: "By coming to men in this form [as a servant] He makes it inescapably clear to them that to accept Him means accepting Him as Lord and that that demands nothing less than the denial of themselves."[10]

There can be little doubt that most persons who enter the professional ministry do so with high motivation and the basic understanding that they are submitting themselves to a ministry that is beyond their own personal strength and resources to perform. The Christian life itself—even apart from the full-time Christian ministry—is a call to endure inhuman stress. "Deny yourself and take up your cross and follow me" is both the offense and the inescapable lure of the gospel. But the power to accomplish that kind of ministry does not come from the Christian. The power to endure is possible only because Christ himself is the Suffering Servant. "I am the vine, you are the branches. . . . Apart from me you can do nothing" (John 15:5). It is possible to face inhuman stress only because the One who calls us has been triumphant. By his power we can deny ourselves to be servants in his name. Ministry that falls short of giving one's life for one's neighbor—whoever that neighbor may be—can hardly claim to be Christian ministry. "But whatever form the Christian ministry takes, the basis is always the same: to lay down one's life for one's friends."[11]

Burned-Out Servants

My specialized ministry as a counselor to pastors brings me into frequent contact with burned-out clergy. Pastor Dan Knowland is typical of many such exhausted ministers. Knowland, forty-four years old, first came to my attention in a three-day working conference. During the breaks and over meals he told me his story. The bishop had relayed various complaints from parishioners that his effectiveness as a parish pastor had diminished sharply over the past eighteen months. People said that Knowland's sermons were poorly constructed and delivered with little conviction. They also reported that he had not been seen much in the community, nor had he been doing much pastoral calling. His ministry in Elk Lake was clearly slipping.

Knowland told me that he had had one "lousy" church assignment after another, and now he was considering secular employment so he could exit from the ministry. He chain-smoked as he complained that he felt like an old man. Lower back pains began to bother him about a year ago. Feeling so much turmoil inside himself, he had difficulty sleeping at night, and frequently awakened before 5:00 A.M. Whenever the telephone rang he got jumpy inside. He claimed that for the past three years he had been too busy to take a vacation.

Typical of Knowland's ministry was an incident that occurred while he was at the conference. He arrived at the 9:00 A.M. session on the third day saying, "I was afraid I was not going to make it here from home." He was unshaven, and it looked like he had not been out of his clothes all night.

"I received a call last night at the motel," he continued, "about 10:30 P.M., from one of the women in my church. Her boss had threatened to lay her off, and she was in a panic. She wanted me to come and talk to her. So I drove the one hundred miles back home and spent the rest of the night talking with her. I left at 6:00 A.M. She had finally calmed down. I think she can now go to work and face her boss. I stopped for coffee on the way back, so I think I am ready now for this final session."

Two days earlier he had told me he feels tired most of the time. All the joy has long ago been drained from his spirit; he dared me to tell him one good thing that he could be happy about in his ministry. Pastor Dan Knowland is a burned-out servant.

Unfortunately, there are too many pastors like Dan Knowland. But the overwhelming message of Protestant Christianity in this country to its clergy is clear: to be an ordained minister one becomes a servant of all, possessed by all, and no longer the possessor of one's own self or one's own soul. It is the message conveyed ever so subtly, and too often not subtly at all, in words like these: "The more of a servant he is, the more he will forget himself and his office as he pours his life into his ministerial functions."[12] This powerful message tells the pastor: "Never be angry, never feel hurt, never want very much money, and never place your own feelings above the feelings of a parishioner!"

One experienced pastor offered this view of ministry: "We are kept priests!" Despite their frequent protests to the contrary, most clergy know what it means to be driven by guilt and hounded by conscience when they fear someone may be displeased with them. The pastor's struggle for self-identity is a running battle with the church as to what obedience to the Lord requires. Who is really in control of the pastor's soul? And just at the moment when the pastor thinks the battle has been won, the words come back with the relentless reminder, "Ministry calls for the denial of yourself; do not listen to your own feelings!"

The purpose of this chapter is to assert that authentic and effective ministry which reflects biblical servant-hood cannot be based upon the popular notion of the "denial of one's self." On the contrary, ministry that has as its purpose to express the love of God and the love of neighbor requires the basic affirmation of one's self and care for one's self. Ministry in the parish for Jesus Christ must begin with the recovery of self by the individual pastor. And the pastor who unashamedly affirms himself or herself will be in the best position for dealing with the multiple stresses of modern ministry.

The Self as the Organizing Center

The root of the crisis in ministry today is with each individual pastor. The question of how to deal with stress will be decided privately as each pastor works toward a clear sense of identity and personal affirmation. And at bottom, the question of dealing with stress in pastoral ministry is a spiritual problem.

John Cobb has offered a viable theological framework for conceptualizing modern ministry. Cobb does not address directly the issue of handling stress in professional ministry, but he holds up for us a model of the structure of Christian existence. Cobb's reflections on the nature of spiritual existence directly apply to the practice of parish ministry.

Cobb has focused his theological writing on the role of the self in the spiritual life. The self he speaks of as the "I"; this is "the center within the psychic life in terms of which the whole is organized."[13] The self is the center. The individual will experience self as the center of one's personality, even as the center of one's being.

For the Christian, according to Cobb, the issue is whether the self will lose its own identity through iden-tification with some aspect of the person such as the will or reason or emotions. In the Christian existence the self transcends all other aspects of the psyche. Indeed the self even transcends itself, taking an objective position in relation to itself. When the self stands back, as it were, and assumes responsibility for itself, it is described by Cobb as spirit. This point is summarized by Cobb: "The self is spirit only when the self as the organizing center transcends the emotions and other aspects of the psychic life."[14] When the self becomes identified with a dominating emotion or desire within one's life, then the self is no longer spirit.

To see how this notion might apply in real life, let us focus on a friend of mine, Pastor Susan Smith, who gave me much concern. She had been a pastor for about nine years, but over the past four to eight months she had become increasingly depressed. Her earlier years of ministry had been quite remarkable. She had distinguished herself through her pastoral leadership in the local church, in the community, and at the judicatory level. Her bishop once described her as certainly one of the most promising of the rising pastors in the conference.

After so many years of enthusiasm and high energy for ministry, Pastor Smith was completely mystified by the unmistakable indications of her deepening depression. She found herself avoiding people for days on end. She had regarded herself as people-oriented in her ministry, and had prided herself on the number of pastoral calls she made. But now, for many days at a time, the last thing she wanted to see was another human face. She retreated to her study and her books. She knew that she was hiding. Other times, she would go home and just sit. Her husband could not figure her out, because she was so unlike her former self.

When I began talking with Pastor Smith about her depression, she was ready to consider leaving the ministry. As we talked, two themes developed from the early years of her life. She recalled that as an adolescent she had had no friends, and had felt isolated from her peers. She felt herself to be quite unattractive, and could not imagine how anyone could like such an undesirable person. When she was fourteen she contracted polio and for several months was near the point of death. Unexplainedly, she recovered. Shortly after that recovery she had a dream in which she was preaching to thousands of people. She determined then that she would be the "best damned preacher there ever was."

The second theme had its roots in her childhood when she was eight years old. Her mother had always told the children that if they ever brought home a D or an F on a report card they would be sent to bed without their supper. If they brought home A's they would receive 50 cents. Susan was a satisfactory student, maintaining a B average. But in third grade she had much difficulty with spelling, and what she feared most did occur. When the report cards were handed to the students, Susan's heart sank when she saw the F for spelling marked in unmistakable red ink.

She was relieved when she came home from school to find her mother preoccupied. She laid the report card on the dining room table and quickly ran outdoors to play. She hoped supper would be concluded before Mother discovered the disastrous report card. However, about a half hour later Susan heard her mother's voice calling from the back door, "Susan! Susan! Come in here right this minute!"

Susan took the punishment that she knew could not be avoided. From that day forward she concluded that (a) even good girls deserve severe punishment, and (b) better girls stand less chance of being punished. Susan has lived a good deal of her life as an eight-year-old, still trying to avoid punishment by being good, and still assuming that whoever is angry with her is certainly right and she is automatically wrong. As a pastor she will do almost anything to avoid conflict because of her dread of the punishment that spells shame, guilt, and rejection to her.

Putting these two themes together, it is quite evident that Pastor Smith has built her ministry around the goal of being the "best damned preacher there ever was" so no one will ever get angry with her. A flawed goal, certainly, but nonetheless the driving motivation behind Susan Smith's ministry.

Pastor Smith's story offers many points at which other clergy can readily identify with her. But what happened to Pastor Smith can be better understood in the light of Cobb's theology of the self. The self, explains Cobb, is spirit when it takes an objective stance toward all aspects of the person's psychic life. That is to say, the self transcends all emotions, desires, and values within the person's life. It stands above and apart so radically that the self is finally responsible even for those aspects of the psyche over which it has no control!

In Pastor Smith's case, the organizing center of her life was not self-transcending self. The organizing center was not spirit. Rather, her self was identified with her obsessive drive to be the world's greatest preacher so she would always be idolized by her parishioners. Consequently her self lost its transcendence over her ministry, and Smith lost her objectivity. She did not belong to herself. She was possessed by her drive to be idolized. Having lost perspective on her ministry, she was terrified by any hint of confrontation, disagreement, or criticism. Any parishioner who expressed the slightest disagreement looked to Smith like an "army"! In a word, she was emotionally overidentified with her self-image as a faultless preacher and minister. With the loss of spirit as the organizing center of her life, she also lost the ability to take charge of her own life. The final step in the process was that ministry lost all its joy and became a meaningless burden.

Dis-identification. Cobb emphasizes that if the human self is to be strengthened as the organizing center for the person, it must be dis-identified from all other aspects of the person's psychic life. Cobb has found the work of Roberto Assagioli to be a useful aid for strengthening the self. Cobb observes, "Assagioli provides us with an effective method for strengthening the spirit."[15] The purpose of Assagioli's method is to make it possible for the self or "I" to objectify the emotions, the reason, even the will, in order clearly to distinguish itself from them.

Now I invite you to take a fifteen-minute break from your reading of this chapter so you can experience theology through an exercise in dis-identification proposed by Assagioli. Put yourself in a comfortable position, relax all parts of your body, and take a few deep breaths. Slowly and thoughtfully make the following affirmation:

> I *have* a body but *I am not* my body. My body may find itself in different conditions of health or sickness; it may be rested or tired, but that has nothing to do with my self, my real "I." My body is my precious instrument of experience and of action in the outer world, but it is *only* an instrument. I treat it well; I seek to keep it in good health, but it is *not* myself. I *have* a body, but *I am not* my body.
>
> I *have* emotions, but *I am not* my emotions. These emotions are countless, contradictory, changing, and yet I know that I always remain I, *my-self,* in times of hope or of despair, in joy or in pain, in a state of irritation or of calm. Since I can observe, understand and judge my emotions, and then increasingly dominate, direct and utilize them, it is evident that *they are not myself.* I *have* emotions, but *I am not* my emotions.
>
> I *have* desires, but *I am not* my desires, aroused by drives, physical and emotional, and by outer influences. Desires too are changeable and contradictory, with alternations of

attraction and repulsion. I *have* desires but *they are not* myself.

I *have* an intellect, but *I am not* my intellect. It is more or less developed and active; it is undisciplined but teachable; it is an organ of knowledge in regard to the outer world as well as the inner; but *it is not myself.* I *have* an intellect, but *I am not* my intellect.

I recognize and affirm that I am a Centre of pure self-consciousness. I am a Centre of *Will,* capable of mastering, directing and using all my psychological processes and my physical body.[16]

Assagioli summarizes the profound sense of self-identity which develops out of this process of dis-identification:

What am I then? What remains after discarding from my self-identity the physical, emotional and mental contents of my personality, of my ego? It is the essence of myself —a center of pure self-consciousness and self-realization. It is the permanent factor in the ever-varying flow of my personal life. It is that which gives me the sense of being, of permanence, of inner security. I recognize and I affirm myself as a center of pure self-consciousness. I realize that this center not only has a static self-awareness but also a dynamic power; it is capable of observing, mastering, directing and using all the psychological processes and the physical body. I am a center of awareness and of power.[17]

Earlier we referred to Pastor Susan Smith, who essentially had failed to dis-identify herself from the roles of superlative preacher and "criticism avoider." It was in the process of consulting with a colleague that Smith began to gain objectivity and reclaim a firmer sense of self from the confinement of those roles. Then her depression began to lift, and she knew she was gaining the new perspective she needed. She retained her gifts as a preacher, and she continued to use sensitivity and wisdom when dealing with conflict, but by "standing back" and looking at the grip those roles had on her life, she dis-identified herself from them, took control, and affirmed her own selfhood.

Many clergy can identify with Pastor Smith as they recognize the deeper motivations that dominate them. They do not then possess themselves, and they are vulnerable to excessive stress. The self is weakened when ministry is organized around drives and needs that own the pastor, instead of the pastor being in charge of these basic motivations.

Ministry based on wholeness. There was a time, explains Cobb, when Christianity focused only on the life of the spirit, to the exclusion of all other aspects of human experience. The intentional abuse of the body through deprivation and inflicted pain have not been uncommon examples in our Christian tradition of attempts to discipline and strengthen the spirit at the expense of the personal and physical life. The day has come, says Cobb, when the spirit no longer needs to continue such a tyranny over the other psychophysical aspects of human life. Christian existence requires that full attention be given to the appropriate place for a strong and healthy body, strong and healthy emotions, a strong and healthy reason, a strong and healthy imagination, a strong and healthy will, besides a strong and healthy spirit.[18]

The Christian life has as its primary goal "wholeness centering in spirit."[19] Such a wholeness is indeed more possible as the self is strengthened in its capacity for making choices. Instead of being captive to drives, urges, emotions, or reason, the self exercises the power of choice so every aspect of one's life can be given its appropriate place and freedom. The stronger the self, the wider will be the range of human experience that can be cultivated and enjoyed. It is the centering, directing power of the self as spirit which offers such a creative possibility.

Cobb, in his work on *Theology and Pastoral Care,* develops his thesis as a rationale for the pastoral goals of clergy in their work among their parishioners. The irony is that clergy need first to apply to themselves the theological views Cobb outlines. For effective stress management, they need to claim for themselves the power of a spiritual existence that strengthens their own selfhood. When ministers have attained the level of spiritual existence described by Cobb, they will have strengthened three fundamental dimensions of their own personal life and ministry.

First, they will have strengthened the power of their own self-identity. It will be more clear to them that they belong to themselves and not to those whom they serve. Secondly, there will be the freedom that comes from greater self-responsibility. The pastor will not need to plead helplessness in any circumstances. Thirdly, the pastor will recognize greater possibilities for being a choice maker. No longer is a pastor under the constraint of "I must . . ." or "I have to . . ." The self as spirit in service to God and Christ is always a chooser from options.

Some of the qualities of ministry that are centered upon spirit were envisioned by Edgar Mills when he originated the idea of the "intentional minister." Intentionality means "purposefully directing one's life as much as possible rather than simply allowing it to be determined by past and present pressures."[20] This means taking an active instead of a reactive posture toward ministry.

> For some, the awareness of being bound by external circumstances and internal limits is an occasional frustration, while for others it is a daily grinding reality. By

contrast, some people do seem more in control of their world, setting goals and achieving them, maintaining directions in spite of barriers. Many of these are *intentional* people. Their experience confirms that, although environmental pressures have to be taken into account, people's own intentionality can, to a large degree, determine the direction and fruitfulness of their lives.[21]

Some may protest that what is being proposed here is simply a radical subjectivism that puts ministry on the shakiest of foundations. Are we not suggesting that the pastor be elevated by the aggrandizement of personal self-esteem? Where is the pastor's connection with the heritage and the traditions of the church? How is the pastor accountable to church structures? Where is the authority of the church if we place all power in the fundamental uniqueness and freedom of individual pastors and their parishioners?

A radical subjectivism is not being proposed here as the theological framework for ministry. Rather, the appropriate role of the self, as developed within Cobb's theological framework, is being affirmed as a viable model for Christian ministry. Moreover, what is being proposed is not altogether new. Paul Scherer, renowned not many years ago as a Lutheran preacher, observed in his Lyman Beecher Lectures at Yale: "You have nothing else but you. Give it reverence and give it freedom. . . . To have a mind of your own is to be another chance for the Kingdom in the hands of God; to have no mind but your own is to be no more than the ghost of that chance forever."[22] Indeed, self that is spirit means having a mind of your own that knows it is in the service of Another!

Caring for Oneself

The basic requirements for adequate mental health, particularly as they apply to clergy, have been known for quite some time.[23] We have been short, however, on an adequate theology for ministry that took account of the mental health needs of clergy. Ordinarily, two clear themes have been signaled to clergy and seminarians. The two contradictory messages have been: "Be a faithful, sacrificing servant," and "You are lacking in wisdom if you wear yourself out and collapse before retirement." Goodykoontz reflects clearly this double message in his highly regarded book on the ministry. Early in his presentation he says: "The Christian is to pour out his life in service as a sacrifice of praise. To be a minister is to be a servant."[24] But then, as if afraid some clergy may take him seriously, Goodykoontz qualifies his argument at the end of his book with this warning:

> The compulsively driven minister who never has any time for his family ought to examine himself before God, and if that does not cause him to slow down, to be less pushed, and to find more time for his family, then he probably needs to consult a good pastoral counselor, or a psychiatrist![25]

Unfortunately, too many pastors have taken to heart the message from the first pages without waiting to read the author's warning at the end.

Strengthening the self and finding wholeness for one's life and ministry is best understood as responsibly *loving and taking care of oneself.* Wholeness centered in spirit for the purpose of loving others is essentially the discipline of *loving and taking care of oneself.* Creative, effective ministry is rooted in the discipline of such a spiritual wholeness!

In the fall of 1974, five thousand Lutherans responded to a questionnaire that was entitled "What Contributes to, What Detracts from Effective Christian Ministries?" The questionnaire contained 461 statements about all the complexities of ministry. Those filling out the questionnaire belonged to five groups. They included laypersons, parish pastors, seminary professors, senior seminary students, and judicatory presidents and executives. Their responses were tabulated and summarized in the recent publication, *Ten Faces of Ministry.* [26] These Lutherans identified necessary pastoral perspectives and ministry skills for effective pastoral leadership. A firm personal faith evident in a pastor's life and ministry was determined to be the most important perspective for ministry.

The second perspective the Lutherans look for in a pastor is that of being a confident person who can nondefensively, actively, reach out and affirm the value of all persons. Speaking to the importance of that quality, the authors of the report declare: "The central issue raised here for pastors is the question of self-love: the degree to which a pastor senses his or her own self-worth. This chapter highlights the very considerable contribution to ministry that a pastor's self-esteem can make." [27] The authors then go on to make this crucial point:

> One way to look at this area of ministry is to consider which way one's decisions habitually tip—toward meeting the needs of others and ignoring or postponing one's own needs, or toward an appropriate respect for one's own needs as well as the needs of others. A pastor may go to a church subcommittee meeting, even though it was called at the last minute, or go ahead with a previous promise to his or her family. When there is a choice, do pastors habitually decide *against* themselves? Perhaps taking account of one or two recent decisions is not so useful

as noticing over time how often they sacrificed their own needs or schedules for others, and how often they were firm about their own needs and schedules. To make the latter choice some of the time is to say, "I'm worth something." Too little self-affirmation of this sort may be a danger signal.[28]

John Harris has recently addressed the question of how pastors can effectively deal with the complex dynamics of congregations that are in conflict and in transition. Examining the irrational forces that can block effective communication between pastors and their parishioners, Harris finally boils the matter down to the pastor's role.

> Certainly, the single most important figure in this complex maze is the pastor. Perhaps this seems an unfair weight to put on one person's shoulders, but I know of no instance in which such forces have been altered against the will of the pastor or without his commitment and help.[29]

Having thus stated how crucial the pastor is, Harris then underscores the heart of the matter. "In many ways, this is the most important point of all I have to make. . . . What our situation requires is pastors with the capacity for autonomy."[30] Harris is careful to state that autonomy for ministry does not mean a crude self-assertion or pointless adolescent rebellion. Autonomy is a person's inner capacity to govern oneself when there must be a balance between one's own needs and values and the demands and needs of the congregation. Autonomy that takes seriously the pastor's own needs is in fact, according to Harris, essential to being a Christian servant.

> It [autonomy] does not contradict the concept of ministry as servanthood, but is its essential accompaniment. In order to sustain a creative degree of tension, to take risks, to be out front about his hopes and intentions, to tolerate

ambiguity, to stand criticism, to challenge prevailing norms—the pastor must have within himself the ability to be an autonomous person. . . .

For Christians, obedience to God does not mean the surrender of self-hood, but a willing commitment of energy, talent, and reason to the purposes of Christ. Refusal to value one's self, on whatever grounds, is false virtue, and may in fact arise out of anxiety as a trick we play in order to force ourselves to abandon the quest for wholeness. In Jesus' parable of the talents, the poor servant is the one who fails to take initiative, to assert his own judgment, and to use what had been given him to advantage.[31]

Self-Affirmation with Self-Emptying

Any adequate attempt to deal with the stress of ministry must begin from a theological framework. We cannot simply offer remedies from a purely psychological perspective. Stress management for clergy is essentially a theological enterprise. The theological model proposed by John Cobb is offered as only one way to take a theological approach to clergy stress.

My experience with pastors in a wide variety of settings has confirmed that an increasing number of clergy are learning to take care of themselves for the sake of their ministry. Some of these pastors have a sophisticated theological rationale for their self-care; others care for themselves in a very natural manner that they seem to take for granted. However, all of them agree on a spiritual understanding that taking care of one's self, one's needs and interests, is the prerequisite to ministry. They assert in their own ways that without the recovery of self, ministry inevitably suffers. For example, Pastor Bynum made a pointed observation about the meaning of Christian humility as it applies to the minister as servant.

Humility is something different from slavery. True humility begins with a rather high appraisal of oneself, that I am worth taking care of, I have value. There is also part of our tradition that says that while we were yet in our sins Christ died for us. That means that there is an intrinsic value and innate possibility within us for revealing the image of our creator. Also it appears to be much easier for God to love us than it is for us to love ourselves. We get messed up when we try to love others without first loving ourselves. One of the neighborly commandments of Jesus, that we gloss over right away, is that we love our neighbor in the way we love ourselves. So some kind of self-esteem has got to be there. We may be more humble, in terms of the basic meaning of humility, when we really do appraise ourselves as having inestimable worth, rights, and goodness.

Pastor Nancy Flynn recognized a pastor's need to be aware of the problem of selfishness and self-centeredness. Her theological reflection gave her a perspective for recognizing the difference between selfishness and taking care of oneself.

If I am a minister trying to help others receive the good life, and I am not taking care of what has been given to me, then that is a real contradiction in my ministry. My life has been entrusted to me, opportunities have been given to me, and I can make use of them. To me that is not selfishness as much as it is an enrichment or sharing. If I do not take care of myself, I have nothing to give, I have nothing to receive with. I am a shell. Selfishness is a hoarding, which does not involve giving and receiving. Selfishness is only one way. I do not see taking care of myself as being all one way; it is give-and-take with other people.

Pastor Charles Taylor has adopted a rule of thumb that he cannot handle more than thirty-five meaningful relationships at any one time. He keeps track of that list and periodically revises it. He wants to be sure that the relationships do not drain him, and to give each relationship the energy that is required. He explains his system: "If I take on a counseling case, someone else has to be dropped from the list." But the most important characteristic of the list is this:

> I also have the list prioritized somewhat, so that I know who is at the top of the list. And I happen to be at the top of the list. First is me. But my feeling is that if I do put myself at the top of the list, I am not hurting anybody else ultimately. They will reap the benefit of my putting myself first. Jesus says, "Love your neighbor as yourself." Before you can really love your neighbor you have to love yourself.

These and other pastors have discovered that servant and self are not mutually exclusive, but instead are mutually dependent upon each other for their full expression in ministry. To attempt to have the servant dimension without self is to become a robot. Tragically, however, there are clergy functioning as robots because long ago they gave up all claim to their own being. Likewise, to have self without the servant dimension is to sacrifice ministry to arrogance. Neither self nor servant alone, without the other, is Christian. Henri Nouwen made the point this way: "Self-affirmation and self-emptying are not opposites because no man can give away what he does not have."[32] Nouwen goes on to underscore the necessity for maintaining the dynamic tension between servant and self: "So the identity of the pastor, as it becomes visible in his pastoral care, is born from the intangible tension between self-affirmation and self-denial, self-fulfillment and self-emptying, self-realization and self-sacrifice."[33] There cannot be ministry in the fullest sense without affirmation of self.

What price shall we continue to pay in the church and in the lives of pastors because the practice of ministry is thought to be possible without self? What is at stake is not just the self-esteem of a few clergy. Besides the personal lives of those clergy are their families and also the congregations which those pastors serve. Pastoral leadership itself, throughout the church, is at stake. It is true that "if clergy fail to be intentional about themselves and their purposes, the intentionalities of others, by default, will become theirs."[34] The price to be paid for the loss of self will be recognized in the loss of effective ministry. In understandable terms Paul Tillich explains the issue facing every pastor.

> Self-loss as the first and basic mark of evil is the loss of one's determining center; it is the disintegration of the centered self by disruptive drives which cannot be brought into unity. So long as they are centered, these drives constitute the person as a whole. If they move against one another, they split the person. The further the disruption goes, the more the being of man as man is threatened. Man's centered self may break up, and, with the loss of self, man loses his world.
>
> Self-loss is the loss of one's determining center, the disintegration of the unity of the person. This is manifest in moral conflicts and in psychopathological disruptions, independently or interdependently. The horrifying experience of "falling to pieces" gets hold of the person.[35]

Ministry requires the recovery and the affirmation of the self, both firmly and dynamically, in every pastor. Then the pastor will be what James Ashbrook calls a "responding-responsible person." Ashbrook continues:

> That means cultivating a heightened sense of I-ness, so that the clergyman experiences himself as subject more than object, as actor more than re-actor. He must respond from a center of inwardness and stop manipulating or being manipulated by himself and others. As

actor, he is a molder of events more than a prisoner of events.[36]

If medical doctor Tobias Brocher is correct in his assertion that "people who are suffering most from stress are those who feel they can't determine their lives," then certainly the "responding-responsible" person is the least vulnerable to being overwhelmed by stress.[37]

The pastors who consciously and without apology take good care of themselves have by far the best chance to be servants of Christ for all the years of their calling.

CHAPTER 3

Personal Resources for Managing Stress

Authentic self-love is not a matter of being curved inward upon the self. It is not narcissism, nor is it a grasping selfishness. It is self-acceptance and affirmation of one's own graciously-given worth and creaturely fineness (in spite of all distortions and flaws). (James B. Nelson)[1]

Solitude is the place of the great struggle and the place of the great encounter. It is the struggle against the compulsions of the false self and the encounter with the loving God who offers himself as the new substance of the new self. (Henri J. M. Nouwen)[2]

Self-care for the strengthening of the human spirit is required at three deeply personal levels of the pastor's life. The spiritual resources of the pastor's faith are a unique asset as the pastor copes with the stresses of ministry. Another vital personal resource, if a pastor is married, is the enrichment that occurs when pastor and spouse consciously cultivate their covenant commitments to each other. Dealing with stress should also take account of the particular interests that motivate creativity and provide meaningful satisfaction for the pastor. Purposeful attention given to these particular areas of one's own life will enhance the pastor's capacity for meeting all the stressful responsibilities of ministry.

The Spiritual Journey

The ministry is the only major profession that without hesitation can discuss spirituality as a principal resource for dealing with stress. When other professionals hold seminars on the issue of burnout, the presentations center around the inhuman demands and the inhuman environments in which the professional must meet those demands. How does a crisis counselor for a human service agency avoid burnout after dealing continuously with one human tragedy after another, week in and week out? How can agencies create an environment in which caseworkers and their administrators can work in a context of mutual understanding without tension and hostility? These are the types of questions professional human service workers ask. But as they search for answers, the personal spiritual dimension in everyone's life that is a unique and vital resource for controlling vocational stress is usually ignored.

Many clergy, however, are recognizing that their spirituality is a primary resource for coping with the pressures of ministry. Pastor Duane Rogers speaks of his own spiritual growth, which gives him a balanced perspective for the parish. Note that first he asserts the need to claim his own self-identity, thus putting distance between himself and the sources of pressure that would overwhelm him:

> I give a tremendous lot. I know that by how physically tired I am on many occasions. What I find is that in taking myself seriously I have more energy to give and there are more resources to spread around. If I spent all my time in my office or within the walls of that one church, I would have very little to give and there would be very little feeding of my fire. So there would be little energy to share with others.

Then he moves on to explain the dynamics of his own spiritual journey. He speaks of a transcendent Self, which in theological language he would call Spirit, or God:

> A great deal of my personal growth is aimed at disclosing this Self to me, of integrating my little self with this big Self, getting us closer together. I know sin and estrangement when the two are not together. I experience grace or salvation when Creator and creature are together, when my little self and my big Self are integrated. The closer I get to this Self, God, the richer I am, the more fulfilled I am, the more I have to offer, and the better minister I am.

Another pastor, Greg Carlson, finds that his spiritual journey requires solitude. He spends several days, sometimes a week, at a retreat center where he can read Scripture, meditate, and pray. Two themes emerge from his description of that process. One theme is the bold affirmation of himself, and the other theme relates to the benefits of gaining new perspectives on his relationships with people. First, he affirms his own needs:

> I see that retreat time as an opportunity. It is pure luxury to take all that time just for myself. I am sure there are a lot of beneficial "slopovers" to other people including my family, the church, etc., but mainly getting away like that really helps me to get renewed. My getting away is at the expense of a lot of people and of church program. You just have to say, if you are serious about getting away by yourself, "I'm more important."

Then he goes on to describe what happens because he has taken that time for his own spiritual journey:

> I am far more patient, when I come back, with difficult people, with the neurotic people who want to take advantage of you. I can deal with them seriously, intensively, and then say, "Go in peace." Then I can move on to

something else. I think that when you're uptight, you have a guilty conscience about how you should have dealt with them. You feel you should have given them more time, or the time you gave them should have been more productive, or you did not help them very much. I tend to brood over personal failure with an individual when I lose the perspective I gain from my periodic retreats.

In God's presence the self receives the strength necessary for ministry. We gain a deeper capacity for love because we begin to see other persons in a new light, despite how exasperating and unlovable they are at times! How essential this spiritual dimension is for dealing with stress!

The movement of the spiritual journey.   Every pastor needs to discover an authentic style of piety that is congruent with his or her own unique spiritual journey. The forms that such practices of devotion can take are limitless. Whatever form a pastor's spiritual journey may follow, the fruits of the journey will be those identified by Paul in Gal. 5:22–23. Those spiritual graces of love, joy, peace, patience, kindness, goodness, faithfulness, gentleness, and self-control identify the persons who can cope with stress because their self-esteem and self-affirmation are bound to God's love in Christ.

Certain aspects of Roman Catholic spirituality have greatly enriched my own understanding of the spiritual journey. A structured week-long Jesuit retreat offered me particular clarity for the strengthening of self for managing stress. From that Jesuit tradition I experienced one of many possible sequences in spirituality, a sequence that has five essential themes.[3]

This particular spiritual journey begins as we *affirm human creaturehood.* Personal spirituality is based in one's primary identity as a child of God. This is essentially a trusting relationship. Erik Erikson has demonstrated the primacy of basic trust in the relationship of the infant to its parents.[4] So, too, the spiritual journey that strengthens the self for ministry is founded upon trust in God's seeking, caring love for those whom God has created.

In realizing one's creatureliness, the self confirms the basic truth about itself. Out of our dependence we first utter the words: "I am. I am meant for communion with God." Augustine's observation that we are restless until we find rest in God is the truth of our creatureliness.[5] And the fundamental fact that undergirds the self for the demands of ministry is that God is the one who takes the necessary steps to find us and call us from our restlessness.

The next step in the spiritual journey is to *acknowledge sin, which is estrangement from the Creator.* Alienation from God is the result of the self being lost in its own self-preoccupation. The self is then faced with the sin either of pride or of despair. However, as the spiritual journey continues in the assurance of God's unconditioned love, the personal, unique, and powerful character of sinfulness can be faced.

And faced it must be. Failure to acknowledge fully our profound estrangement from God is the primary source of all stress in human life. This is the case because until we recognize the reality of our estrangement, we do not have the necessary perspective for recognizing the essential priorities and values needed in our lives. John was clear about this when he said, "If we say we have no sin, we deceive ourselves, and the truth is not in us" (I John 1:8). Without that truth, what is trivial takes on immense importance, and the matters of true significance elude us. No wonder, then, we are overcome by stress of our own making!

The third step in the spiritual journey is to *respond to Jesus Christ.* He who is the Subject of the Gospels invites us, through him, to live beyond our selves. Ministry cannot be endured without first making a wholehearted response to that invitation. For it is the promise that we shall live beyond our selves that strengthens the self beyond its own resources. Making the response to Jesus Christ is the step that begins to move us out of our own self-preoccupation. That is the salvation which holds the possibility for us to be free to love others. Then the self is strengthened because it is fulfilling the purpose for which it was originally created!

Next in the spiritual journey, *affirm God's incredible love,* demonstrated by Jesus' suffering and death. In the death of Christ the self is confronted with the depths to which God must go to liberate the self from its own preoccupation. Here the self encounters the final freedom promised through love. The final freedom from self-preoccupation is not denial of the self, but rather the turning of the self outward in total self-giving for neighbor and friend. The love that dies on the cross affirms its own power as it suffers in the place of others and for others.

This theme is found not only in narratives recounting Jesus' death but in Old Testament passages as well. These passages include Isa. 52:13 to 53:12: "Surely he has borne our griefs and carried our sorrows; yet we esteemed him stricken, smitten by God, and afflicted" (Isa. 53:4). The spiritual journey reaches its more intensely personal focus when the self knows itself to be lovable, for with God the miracle is that each person is so loved. Ministry must begin with that truth being affirmed continually within the pastor's own life!

The final step of the spiritual journey is to *live beyond self-preoccupation.* The self strengthened for ministry has a risen Lord! It is through the personal relationship with God as Lord that the self is able to live from the freeing perspective of spirit. An objective viewpoint becomes possible toward all the thoughts, passing feelings or emotions, social roles, urges, and drives that can become so burdensome and so inhibiting to ministry. It is possible for the Christian to obey the injunction "Do not be conformed to this world" (Rom. 12:2) because the risen Lord shall never be conformed to this world.

The resurrection guarantees new life for the self. Without the power of the risen Christ, the self is vulnerable to the pressures and emotions that threaten its essential integrity. The resurrected Lord brings assurance and hope that the self within each person shall not be overwhelmed by stress, but rather shall be free to live as spirit and free to live for others. "Thanks be to God, who gives us the victory through our Lord Jesus Christ." (I Cor. 15:57)

Matthew Fox, a Dominican priest writing about spirituality for Protestants, offers us the test for assessing our spiritual journey.

> The authentic test of our and others' and our society's claims to spirituality is *creative compassion*. . . . I mean the burning passion of lived awareness that we occupy a precarious existence on this planet together with the soil and its flowers, the water and its fishes, the air and its birds, the fire and energy sources; that our fellow human beings are truly brothers and sisters with whom it is better always to make love-justice than war; and that gentleness lasts longer and touches more deeply than other kinds of power. By "creative" I mean the commitment to giving birth to this kind of awareness where we live, work, play and pray.[6]

Pastors who need fresh resources for coping with stress should explore new approaches for enlivening their own spiritual journey. The self that confidently manages stress *for* ministry will do so from a lively spirituality that has a creative and dynamic compassion in its ministry to others.

For Married Pastors

Marriage should not be thought of as a normal or necessary state for clergy. However, those pastors who are married have in their marriage and their family life resources for coping with stress that can hardly be found elsewhere.

Lutherans have clearly recognized the positive contribution that the pastor's family life makes to ministry. In a Lutheran study, reported in *Ten Faces of Ministry,* of the long list of characteristics that five thousand Lutherans said they desire in a pastor, commitment to family was third, coming after the pastor's maintenance of a personal devotional life and the pastor's confidence in Christ's Lordship. "A pastor whose primary support group is a lively, joyously, and affirmatively interacting family has a great asset in ministry."[7]

The authors of that Lutheran study see a direct link between a pastor's capacity to love and care for herself or himself and how the pastor cares for the family. Shortchanging one's family is not in the best interests of the church. "Those who consistently and regularly sacrifice their own needs often extend that expectation to their families, sacrificing their needs as well. This kind of shortsighted unselfishness can have bitter long-term results."[8]

In *Ten Faces of Ministry* the authors cite the experience of a Pastor Severson, who never set any limits but always made himself available for any church obligation. He graciously picked up the slack for others and stayed late into the night for those meetings which pick up after the regular meeting has adjourned. He would think nothing of interrupting dinner or postponing a family shopping trip so he could attend to "important" matters in the congregation. This pattern of dutiful service went on for ten or fifteen years before the oblivious pastor Severson noticed that his wife and his teen-age children had learned how to carry on their lives without him—because of necessity they had learned how to do that. Pastor Severson, in the name of Christian ministry, had become an outsider in his own marriage and his own family. The authors comment: "To have estranged oneself from one's family—one's most close and lasting support group—is to have wandered unawares into a very lonely place."[9]

My personal experiences with clergy of all denominations directly confirm this observation. The pastor who reports a basic high level of satisfaction in marriage is in the best position to cope with demanding levels of daily stress and to do effective work as a pastor. The reverse is also true. The pastor who experiences various levels of dissatisfaction, friction, or tension at home will ordinarily face correspondingly diminished levels of effectiveness in pastoral work. Some pastors try to pretend that they can seal off their personal life and their disruptive home life from their professional functioning. That, however, is an illusion of the naive!

Reserving time for marriage and family. Clergy who recognize a significant change for the better in the way they now relate to their families invariably point to their having learned to say no. For many pastors this is the most difficult lesson. Greek and Hebrew or church history were never as hard as learning how to say no. Somehow, pastors can imagine the worst of consequences should they utter that two-letter word. In fact, one pastor only began to say no when he was about to lose his family. He now has boundaries in his life for the first time.

> I can draw boundaries now, boundaries in terms of what I expect of myself and what I am able to give of myself.

I now have boundaries about what I will let somebody else put on me. Besides, I have learned that I can never do the work which others need to do for themselves.

Since learning to set those boundaries in his ministry he has recovered a rich marital relationship that he came very close to losing.

Another pastor learned something important when his first child was born. His wife reported having contractions a week and a half earlier than expected. Suddenly it was necessary to take her to the hospital at about 8:30 in the morning. She continued in labor all through the day, and their daughter was born at 10:30 in the evening. Because of this unplanned interruption in his schedule, all his "important" pastoral appointments had to be abruptly canceled for the entire day. To his surprise, nothing fell apart because he was not there.

Now he has requested that the governing board of the congregation hold all its committee meetings on one of two specific nights in the month. On those two evenings two or three committees meet, and he "floats" between the committee meetings. His officers appreciate this efficiency, and it enables him to avoid attending five different committee meetings on five different nights each month. Result: he has more time with his family. He has concluded, "My schedule does not interfere with my family life unless I let it."

Another experienced pastor suggested to his governing board that all committee meetings be held at the church on Sunday morning right after the worship service. His lay leaders did not want to come out on weeknights either, so they were quite receptive to his suggestion. He also arranges his weekday schedule so that he is always home by 3:00 P.M. in order to spend the latter half of the afternoon with his children. His rationale for designing his ministry with this type of structure is directly related to his family. "If I cannot care for the primary covenant in my life, namely my family, then how can I really be expected to adequately meet the needs of other persons? If I fail in my covenant with my family, the same flaws will occur in other relationships, too."

A pastor explained how he and his wife went away for a weekend, just to be by themselves. Though they regularly have taken such a weekend away every winter, he had not received specific permission from his governing board to be away this particular time. Nonetheless, he asked the associate pastor to take all the responsibilities for preaching that Sunday, and other persons were alerted to take care of the responsibilities that the pastor usually carried for the adult Sunday school class. Otherwise, no explanation was given to the congregation to account for the absence of the pastor and his wife. They were just gone. The pastor explained that he knows his church officers would applaud his getting away, because they know the hours he works. Furthermore, he said, "I just feel I have it coming, like any ordinary human being who wants a weekend away. I was doing the work of the Kingdom taking care of myself and my wife."

One pastor reluctantly admitted that at one time in his ministry he was away from the family forty-five evenings in a row! Another pastor has determined that this will not happen to him because each Sunday he blocks out his weekly schedule and sees to it that his family has first priority, first claim on his time. That way his wife and his children know that they—not the church—are first in his life.

Such an example from the pastor sends an important message to the congregation. The message to the parishioners indicates that all professional people should keep their priorities straight. One minister made the following comment:

I see payoff for ministry in the model that I am setting for the young families who have one or two professional members. They see that I recognize how important it is to spend time with my family, quality time in meaningful blocks. When I am with my family, other parents see me living the gospel instead of only talking it.

The feelings of most of these pastors were summed up by the female minister who said: "Being close to my family leaves me a wholistic person. If I am feeling whole about myself, if I am feeling O.K. about my relationship to my family, then I feel the part of me that I can give to the parish is whole."

Taking a serious look at your marriage. Lederer and Jackson, in *The Mirages of Marriage,* have correctly observed: "Relationship is a process involving constant change; and constant change requires the spouses to *keep working on their relationship until the day they die.*"[10] In order for a pastor and spouse to maintain dynamic growth in their relationship, a thorough analysis of their marriage should be undertaken periodically by both spouses together.[11]

Lederer and Jackson have proposed that such an examination be done by both spouses privately, or by talking together, or perhaps by having a nonprofessional third party assist in the process. Such an analysis should take an honest look at all aspects of the marriage. No doubt there are some areas more sensitive than others, like an exposed raw nerve. Other areas will be a source of joy and satisfaction for both partners. Lederer and Jackson have suggested a list of probing questions that marriage partners can discuss with each other in order to assess their relationship. Ten of those questions are offered here:[12]

1. Do you look forward to rejoining your spouse after being separated during the day?
2. In terms of Harry Stack Sullivan's definition of the state of love *("When the satisfaction or the security of another*

person becomes as significant to one as is one's own satisfaction or security, then the state of love exists"), [13] do you love your spouse?—is the security and well-being of your wife or husband as significant to you as your own security and well-being?

3. Using this same definition, does your spouse love you?
4. Who do you believe is exerting the greater effort to make the marriage successful, you or your spouse? Give reasons for this answer.
5. Have you considered the possibility of a divorce, even as a fleeting thought?
6. Knowing what you do now about your present marriage, would you—if you were again single—still marry the same person?
7. Is your married sex life satisfactory?
8. What behavior or techniques on the part of your spouse would make your sex life more satisfying?
9. If you have children, do they seem to you to help or to hinder your marriage? If you could begin your marriage all over, and be without children, would you prefer to have none?
10. List five reasons why your marriage is advantageous (or satisfying) for you.

If a couple uncovers deep hurts that cannot be worked through in the process of answering these ten questions, professional help and guidance should be sought. Failing to seek professional help when one knows it is needed invites years of tension that wear on both individuals, besides draining energy away from the ministry. Many clergy fear going to a professional counselor or therapist out of concern that the community will decide that the pastor is "sick." Also, pastors may resist going to another professional because of the discomfort of asking for help instead of being the helper. Though clergy should be careful where they seek help, it is no longer justified for pastors and their family members to avoid professional assistance. There are adequate resources for therapy and counseling within financial and geographical reach of most clergy families. Some of the professional resources available to pastors are outlined in Chapter Six.

The pastor lives under a tragic illusion who believes that to do a better job of ministry requires sacrificing family relationships. Ministry is enriched when the pastor finds wholeness at home. Any pastor who chooses to disregard that truth greatly imperils any chance of claiming a dynamic sense of self that is rooted in spirit and supported by loving relationships. Though ministry and marriage can appear to be conflicting covenants, Gaylord Noyce is right in his conclusion:

> The deepening ties of a good marriage provide a school for much of our growth in competence as good pastors. Here is the loving resource for the healthy self we use as counselors and spiritual guides for others. The covenants of marriage and ministry are often in tension, and in apparent conflict. Working through and working within the dilemma may be one of the best assignments we have for learning the Christian life of faithfulness to God.[14]

Discovering and Using One's Major Interests

Many pastors find it difficult to talk about their own interests. They believe that what genuinely interests them does not matter very much, or certainly could have little to do with the practice of ministry. After all, is there not just one way to do parish ministry? Get up at 7:00 A.M. and get to the office by 9:00. Have devotions, open the mail, and study for the sermon. Answer a few letters. Home for lunch. In the afternoon call in the hospitals and see a few shut-ins. Home by 5:00. Eat supper and go out at 7:00 for a meeting. Home again by 10:15, just in time to unwind a few minutes watching Johnny Carson's monologue. And so it will be tomorrow, also. Not much question of whether one enjoys that routine, or what there is about the routine that could possibly be changed for variety or excitement. Is that not simply the way one is supposed to do ministry, day in and day out, year in and year out? Yes, of course, if you want to die of boredom!

There is a better way. It begins with discovering one's major interests. Many persons have never seriously considered all the areas in which they have major interests. The Strong-Campbell Interest Inventory, used by career counselors for identifying areas of interest, is informative because it tells us that we may have developed interests in any one of over twenty different areas.[15] For example, consider outdoor and physical activities where one's interests may broadly include agriculture, nature, adventure, military, and mechanical activities. If one is academically oriented, interests may include science, mathematics, medical science, and medical service. Many clergy have interests in the arts, which include music, dramatics, art, and writing. Pastors also like to relate to people, so many have interests in teaching, social service, athletics, the domestic arts, and religious activities. A person who is more of an "entrepreneur" and likes to be persuasive will likely have interests in public speaking, law and politics, merchandising, sales, and business management. Finally, for those who prefer the environment of an office, office practices may be a major source of interest.

Richard Bolles has suggested another approach for identifying one's chief interests.[16] He proposes that we imagine being at a party in a room with six corners. Suppose that persons with the same interests gravitate with their refreshments to the same corners (which is usually the case). In the first corner are the people who enjoy athletic or mechanical activities, preferring to work with objects, machines, tools, plants, or animals, or to be outdoors. In the next corner is a group of people who like to observe, learn, investigate, analyze, evaluate, or solve problems. Let us go across the room now—stopping a moment for more crackers and cheese.

In the third corner are the people who like to work with data and details, and who enjoy following through on others' instructions. In the fourth corner we can talk with persons who enjoy working with other persons. Usually they can be seen influencing, persuading, performing, leading or managing a group or organization. There are still two more groups, one at each end of this six-cornered room. At the near end we find those who have artistic interests, those who enjoy being innovative and working in unstructured situations, relying on their imagination or creativity. At the far end we find the people who enjoy working with other persons in order to train, inform, enlighten, or cure them. They like to do helpful things for others.

It is important to recognize the distinction between *abilities* and *interests*. We may have particular skills or abilities, but not derive much pleasure from using them. By the same token we may have major interests in areas where our abilities are mediocre or worse. I read about a distinguished medical doctor who was applauded for his lectures to medical students but who, to his own surprise, found greater enjoyment in fixing the plumbing on his kitchen sink, though it took him hours to do what would have taken a professional plumber forty minutes.[17]

In my home there are two children, both males, about four years apart in age. Because their mother and I wanted to be good parents, we bought a trumpet six years ago so that both our sons could receive a musical education through the public school system. We were certainly gratified, even a little proud, when the first son was selected for the all-district school band, and the second son distinguished himself in just his first year of trumpet lessons. Both sons had the ability, even the skill, to play a trumpet, but it was not long before their interest in the trumpet dropped to absolute zero! There may be many reasons, but the fact now remains that neither of our sons has any desire whatsoever to play a trumpet. We now have a slightly used trumpet for sale at our house.

What happened to my sons is true for many persons. One's interests are not always in the areas where there is evidence of ability. However, as a rule, abilities will begin to develop along the lines of one's major interests. In order to manage the stress in one's life more effectively, it is essential that one become increasingly aware of the full range of his or her own varied interests, of what is challenging, exciting, fulfilling. For when one is engaged, whether as a spectator or as a participant, in the activities of one's major interests, a creative power is released that infuses all dimensions of one's life. And thus a greater sense of wholeness is achieved for enlivening and strengthening the self as spirit.

Frequently a pastor who is depressed or discouraged about ministry comes to life as he relates to me the excitement of his hobby or avocation. For one pastor, it was his interest in the circus, its history, the famous performers, as well as the drama of the circus, that had brought so much fun to his life over the years. All the information he shared with me about the circus was striking evidence that what he was relating was a source of renewal and excitement for him. For still another pastor, it was his work with model railroading. In fact, he had attracted local notice as a builder of train layouts. Their special interests not only made these two pastors quite unique persons but also helped them to spend creative and refreshing hours of renewal away from the tensions and pressures of their ministries. Their interests brought forth a dimension and richness of life that otherwise would have been lost. Defining and cultivating one's compelling interests is a prerequisite for a ministry that is not dominated by stress.

Pastor Filson had learned, after going through a period of serious depression, that his interests held the key to his life and his ministry. Indeed, developing his primary interests became, without apology, the principal thrust of his life; his ministry was secondary for him. "The bottom line of my life is personal growth," he explains. As a spinoff, the parish reaps the fruits of his creativity. To recover his own personal sense of self, he finds it necessary to withdraw and be completely by himself. In the winter, pounding nails and studding out the basement is a special interest that renews him. In the summer, gardening restores his creative processes.

> When I garden I feel that I am more whole than much of the time in the parish ministry. Ministry draws so much on just my head. But the gardening allows me to use my hands and my knees. I plant seeds in the earth, and at the same time whatever grows inside my head grows naturally. While I am gardening it is not unusual for a sermon to write itself in my head, spontaneously unfolding!

Following our interests in ministry and allowing them to renew us is the creative potential of self-care. Enduring stifling conformity is the price too many pastors pay when they become immobilized by guilt about being a little different from every other minister. Consider Pastor Betty Nelson's story.

> One thing I think about myself is that I am a creative person. So something that I did that I found was really helpful was to take pottery classes. I actually took time out during the working day. I felt somewhat guilty about that. I was not sure what the parishioners would think as I went over with my little bucket to class in my blue jeans. But I found that was really helpful to me, because the creative part of me was being engaged. That saved me from feeling really frustrated. Therefore, I did not have to

do my creative number on the people who did not want that in the church. It was really freeing! I was me! I just went and thoroughly enjoyed learning how to throw a pot!

But walking down the street to go throw a pot was not a simple matter. She had to struggle seriously with her guilt.

I had to really do some thinking [before deciding] that it was O.K. for me to take the pottery class in the middle of the afternoon. I had to remind myself that I was working X number of hours every night so I ought to be able to take off a couple of hours in the afternoon to take the class.

In how many other thousands of little ways does guilt and the anticipated disapproval of others inhibit pastors from discovering the wider ranges of their unique interests?

When we talk about interests and creativity we are not talking about writing a book of poetry or the great American novel! Creativity through one's interests means finding fulfillment and satisfaction by bringing to life what expresses one's inner self. I once had a colleague in ministry who had a major interest in producing a newsletter once a month. My friend was quite different in his interest from most clergy, who want to spend as little time as possible writing a newsletter. Not only did he write twelve or sixteen pages a month for the newsletter, but he oversaw every step of its production. He usually did the mimeographing of each page, and he personally participated in the stapling and preparation for mailing. He received some recognition for the fine quality of the newsletter, but that was beside the point. For him, it was a creative act that expressed a major interest.

Every person has potential for creativity, because each

of us is unique. Failure to find the richness of that truth in one's life is to lose a major opportunity for strengthening one's own self-affirmation. *Our special interests, usually different from those of our neighbor, are the singular doorway to the power of fulfilling self-expression.* Martin Buber saw this potential for all of us:

> Every person born into this world represents something new, something that never existed before, something original and unique. It is the duty of every person . . . to know . . . that there has never been anyone like him in the world, for if there had been someone like him, there would have been no need for him to be in the world. Every single man is a new thing in the world and is called upon to fulfill his particularity in this world.[18]

The major question is how much of a pastor's time and effort involves areas of principal interest. If the answer is 65 percent or less, that pastor is experiencing too much frustration or boredom at work. As the percentage of creativity and high interest time goes *down,* the percentage of stressful time *goes up.* The fires of creative renewal can only be lighted by the interests that truly excite us.

Responsibly taking care of oneself for ministry requires taking seriously one's areas of primary interest. All parish pastors have to do what James Glasse has called "paying the rent." That is to say, there are basic needs in every congregation that the parish pastor cannot avoid. Glasse lists them as (1) preaching and worship, (2) teaching and pastoral care, and (3) organization and administration. He adds: "I am convinced that a pastor who delivers these basic services has 'paid the rent' in the parish. What he and the parish must understand is that 'paying the rent' is not a full-time job."[19] In other words, there should be quite a lot of room for each pastor to design a pattern of ministry that allows for significant periods of time to be invested in the areas of greatest interest and enjoyment.

The wisest approach for a bored pastor is to brain-storm about how the job description could be redesigned to increase the periods of high interest and enthusiasm. After doing this brainstorming, one should approach the pastor-parish relations committee to discuss how the pastor's particular interests can best match the needs of the congregation. On that basis mutual priorities can be negotiated for the congregation's mission and the pas-tor's ministry. It is certainly to the congregation's advan-tage for the pastor to be doing rewarding work, and that will most likely occur in the areas of ministry that evoke the greatest interest and excitement. In the long run it is better to negotiate these priorities with one's congrega-tion, so the officers can hear their pastor's needs, and so the pastor does not ignore what the leaders feel are the principal needs for the mission of the congregation.

It should be clear that the enjoyment of one's chief interests belongs in both work time and leisure time. If highly satisfying interests are developed only in work but not in leisure, or mostly in leisure but not in work, then there is the risk of a serious loss of balance and wholeness. To preserve that balance, Richard Bolles recommends the principle of alternating rhythm:

> In deciding what to do with your leisure, "the principle of alternating rhythm" suggests that your leisure comple-ment your work . . . , in which case, look at your oldest and most enjoyed skills. If your work does not satisfac-torily employ them, choose leisure activities which will. If your work does satisfactorily employ them, then you may use your leisure to explore your newest and poten-tially most enjoyable skills.[20]

Exploring the wider dimensions of one's own special interests is essential for having the kind of balance to one's ministry that keeps daily pressures within manageable limits. Pastors, however, should watch for evidence within themselves of unnecessary guilt because their interests do not exactly fit someone else's stereotype of the "typical minister." To cope more effectively with stress, pastors will keep in mind that ministry begins at the personal level where the self is strengthened through the continuing spiritual journey, through family and marital relationships, and through the interests and activities that generate deep satisfaction and renewal. Now the next step is to examine resources for managing stress by setting the practice of ministry within appropriate limits.

CHAPTER 4

Ministry Within Limits

This land of ours is full of workaholics. The workaholic's way of life is considered in America to be at one and the same time *(a)* a religious virtue, *(b)* a form of patriotism, *(c)* the way to win friends and influence people, and *(d)* the way to be healthy, wealthy, and wise. Therefore, the workaholic, plagued though he be, is unlikely to change. Why? Because he is a sort of paragon of virtue. He is the one held up as an example by the little old ladies who tell boys and girls how to live. He is the one chosen as "the most likely to succeed." (Wayne E. Oates)[1]

If his love has willingly inclined itself to us, surely it is not aroused by works. (John Calvin)[2]

We have examined self-care at three personal levels of the pastor's life, namely: one's spiritual journey, marriage and family, and major interests. We now turn to sources of stress in the pastor's professional life, and will suggest ways of self-care in these areas. In this chapter we will be concerned with reducing one's need to be a messiah, and with unraveling the complexities of pastoral responsibility. Self-care is essential in these areas of professional functioning if stress in ministry is to be effectively managed. Ministry which recognizes that there are essential limits to the pastor's energy and the pastor's responsibility will be less vulnerable to overburdening pressures.

Scripture Speaks of Only One Messiah

Nostalgia began to rise in Pastor Jim Calder as he and his wife, Gloria, drove again through the familiar shaded main street of Centerville. There was Bart Naylor's gas station over on the corner, and Bart was sitting in his old chair in the shade. Jim waved and was pleased that Bart recognized him and waved back. "Doesn't look like old Bart has changed in the past year," Jim observed to Gloria. "No," she responded, "nor has any of the town. Those were certainly good years we had here."

"They were five tough years, but I can't think of a better place to have started my ministry," Jim reminisced. "The people were always so supportive, and seemed always to be behind whatever I wanted to do. I don't know of anyone who ever said, 'No, don't do that.' Frankly, Gloria, I don't know of any of my seminary classmates who had their first church written up in our denominational magazine as we did two years ago. The community outreach program I developed here, despite all the hard work, was a model that many other churches across the country found they could use, too. I think my being president of the school board helped both the church members and the community to recognize that there was a job to be done here in Centerville, and that we could all work together. It really feels good to come back one year later just to see how things are going now. I bet their budget has topped $95,000 this year, because I had increased it $30,000 in just the five years we were here."

"There's the church and the parsonage," exclaimed Gloria as Jim turned the car off Third Street and proceeded up Elm Avenue. "It looks the same, doesn't it? I wonder if Barbara enjoyed the tulips I planted before we moved out."

"Barbara and Gary are terrific people," Jim answered.

"I can't think of anyone else I would have wanted to follow me here at First Church. Gary has the sensitivity and the enthusiasm to keep the people involved in the programs I started. I wish Gary and Barbara could have been here to see us today, but"—Jim explained—"they are on vacation these two weeks. Bill Sorenson, the new president of the church board, wrote and said he would be here at the church, in the office, today."

Jim brought the car to a stop in front of the church building. "Let's go in and find Bill. That looks like his car in the parking lot."

Jim and Gloria went into the church they had been so familiar with for five years. They found their way quickly back to the office, and after warm greetings and hugs for Pat Hawkins, the church secretary, Jim and Bill went into the parlor and began talking about all that had happened in the church during the past twelve months. Finally, Jim asked Bill, "How are the church's youth programs and the community outreach program going?"

Bill's response hit Jim like a thunderclap. Ten years later Bill's words were still seared across Jim's memory. Bill's face took on a somber expression. After some long moments Bill began, choosing his words carefully. "Jim, while you were here and we were promoting all those wonderful programs, we all thought the congregation was generating those ideas and giving the leadership to get them off the ground. But since you left, and even after Gary and Barbara had arrived, the youth programs and the outreach program have slowed to a stop. With Gary's leadership we hope to find a new purpose, or perhaps find our purpose as a congregation for the first time."

The impact of Bill's words that day turned Jim's ministry completely around. Years later Jim recalled the resolution that he made the moment he heard Bill's words.

I said to myself, "I'll never again do that. I'll never again push my own agenda, no matter how good or important it is." If it is simply my thing, then it saps all my energy. I was just beat when I left that church. I was physically worn out, and for what? I had been the only servant. I did the servant work, though of course I called myself the enabler, the catalyst.

Ernest Becker has observed that all of us are driven by the need to be heroic. It is one way to deal with the ultimate reality that still confounds us, our death. Certainly the drive to be heroic is a common characteristic of many clergy. Though these pastors would deny it, anyone looking at their ministry would easily conclude that the final success of the Kingdom of God depends on the pastor orchestrating all that happens at First Church. Becker's analysis obviously reflects a secular understanding of the human condition. But maybe for that reason it contains insights that we ordinarily would not consider.

Becker crystallizes the issue for all who have any tendency toward being heroes and messiahs:

> The question that becomes then the most important one that man can put to himself is simply this: how conscious is he of what he is doing to earn his feeling of heroism? I suggested that if everyone honestly admitted his urge to be a hero it would be a devastating release of truth.[3]

The crux of the matter, the primary motivation to heroism, according to Becker, is the human struggle with the final fact of life which is the most absurd fact of all —human finitude. Created only a little less than God, humanity is haunted every day by the specter of death. It is the ultimate paradox:

> We might call this existential paradox the condition of *individuality within finitude.* . . . Man is literally split in two: he has an awareness of his own splendid uniqueness in

that he sticks out of nature with a towering majesty, and yet he goes back into the ground a few feet in order blindly and dumbly to rot and disappear forever.[4]

Heroism, the achievement of the extraordinary, is the final human effort to transcend the human. Theologically, it is the effort of human beings to escape the despair of preoccupation with their own finitude.

The achievement of the remarkable is woven thread-and-fiber through our American culture. Indeed, it is patriotic to achieve new records and attain new heights. Each new record reinforces the myth that finitude can be rolled back by every second that is taken off the old record for the mile run or the Boston Marathon. And certainly the ministry, as much as any profession, has unlimited opportunities on a daily basis to attain the remarkable, to perform as the surrogate messiah until the genuine Messiah comes. Perhaps the chief temptation clergy have is to delude themselves with the notion that in First Chruch they are doing for God what God cannot do without them. And do the people not call such a pastor "Wonderful Counselor!" (Isa. 9:6)—or at least "wonderful"?

It takes a lot of energy to be wonderful. And when the energy has been exhausted it is called burnout. Then the people all ask themselves, "How could such a wonderful pastor be burned out?"

Pastor Gregory Dalby has a thought on that question. He marvels at some of his colleagues in ministry. He knows that he is not at his best when he is functioning as a worn-out messiah.

The problem with seeing yourself as a messiah is that you operate under the false assumption that your strength is God's strength, and then you fail to take seriously your own needs for rest and recuperation. I have noticed that issue for me particularly in terms of counseling. I am not pleased by the kind of counseling that I have been able to do, and part of it is that my motor is always running too fast. I do not have the internal peace to be able to sit and listen. Being frantically busy puts a kind of psychic pressure on you that does not permit the personal ease that is required to be empathetic. In the first place I am too defensive. I do not want to deal with any more hurts. I am too busy to have somebody come in and bleed on my carpet.

Is it possible that a messiah could become so busy doing Kingdom work that there would be no energy left over for helping people?

Being a messiah is not taking care of oneself. Practicing heroics day in and day out is not ministry. At its worst it is an attempt to manipulate people; at its best it is still a denial of one's basic humanity and finitude.

Pastor Charles Fleming reflected on the excessive levels of stress in his ministry and blamed himself as well as his seminary training. First, he pointed out that he had been reared as a "preacher's kid," where care for one's self was never modeled by his parents. All his father said by way of giving his son advice was, "Just love your people." Pastor Fleming knew that such advice contained much wisdom, but he did not realize that he needed also to love himself and to care for himself. So, not giving himself and his own needs proper consideration, he set out to keep everyone in his congregation happy.

Besides the modeling he had received from his home, Pastor Fleming recalled his training in seminary ten years earlier.

The seminary mouthed the importance of taking care of yourself, but was still focusing on the people and your role as the pastor to serve the people. I really think we were trained to walk in Jesus' footsteps without ever making any distinction about the uniqueness of our walking as opposed to how Jesus did it. It was not suggested that Jesus had done it his way, and that we would do our ministry our way. The replica of little messiahs was thrust on us. And I accepted all that.

For some pastors, the messianic role of continually striving to be wonderful blends subtly and imperceptibly with their whole personality. For others there is a remarkable change of character as they walk, even just fifty feet, from the parsonage to the church. For those pastors, it is like walking from the bullpen to the pitcher's mound with the eyes of the world and all of the world's burdens resting on them alone. For others it is a matter of pumping themselves up in order to put on another show, bigger and better than the last one.

An increasing number of pastors are caring for themselves and realizing that being a messiah is not a viable approach to ministry. Pastor Ronald Michalson is such a person. As long as I have known him I have been aware that there is no pretense about him. There is nothing splashy or showy about him. That quality may in fact prevent him from attaining what some call success in the ministry—the large church with a large budget. But one is left feeling that here is a pastor who will not likely get in the way of God working through him. He asserts, "I recognize that I am who I am, that I am not Jesus Christ." His congregation is fortunate to have a pastor who knows the difference. He continues:

> I have felt and observed in some of my colleagues at times a kind of messiah complex, [the feeling] that they have to be the ones bringing in the Kingdom, so to speak. But I know that I am a unique person, and that I have particular gifts, particular strengths and weaknesses, and that it is O.K. to be me.

How do we explain that some pastors are able to base their ministry on an unpretentious confidence that affirms their own selfhood, their own humanity, as basically adequate for ministry? Certainly a pastor must incorporate his or her own finiteness into ministry as a fact of life. If, as Becker suggests, human heroics are the human attempt to deal with the absurdity of death, then to affirm one's finitude may be the only Christian response for declaring that no human effort can solve the problem of death. So Pastor Michalson does not have to be a messiah, he does not have to be heroic. He affirms himself for who he is, and is thus freed to point to the One who he is not—Jesus Christ. He cares for himself and keeps the theological priorities of his ministry straight. When asked how he does this, he responded:

> I just do what I feel I must do, and try to live in response to my understanding of the gospel. I recognize my own strengths and weaknesses, and I discover that that is O.K. Others still continue to accept me. Some don't accept me, but that's O.K., too. It doesn't throw me. I have found that if I am honest about who I am and can express how I feel, what my concerns are, what my strengths and limitations are, I am able to have a relationship with most people. I don't have to pretend I have all the answers, because I don't have all the answers.

To care for themselves, pastors must abandon all messianic behavior and affirm that the ministry is the work of the whole church, the ministry of all of God's people. Most pastors know that as a principle, and probably even preach it. But how often is it evident when it comes to the practice of ministry? One pastor facetiously summed up the task of professional ministry by comparing it to that of a successful police force: you simply have to create the illusion of omnipresence. Creating such an illusion motivates heroics in the parish.

The pastor who has the courage to give up illusions of omnipresence will be participating in a shared ministry. It will be shared because the pastor will not be living a life-style that generates false expectations in the parishioners. Rather, a style of ministry that is congruent with the pastor's humanness enables both people and pastor to experience the frustrations and the joys of ministry. Pastor Peter Todd said he could have it no other way:

> There is something beautiful in ministry. There is the counseling and the caring. In that ministry there is a lot of healing. There is a beauty in that. There is also the beauty of being at the front leading a worship service. I get special feelings up there. Sometimes when I am standing a foot from the altar, and everybody is singing the doxology, the hair can crawl on the back of my neck. There is something special about that. If I stop being the messiah, and they are also taking part in leading the worship and in the caring and healing parts of the ministry, my parishioners can also share in the hair standing up on the back of their necks and the joy of seeing somebody healed or the joy of seeing somebody grow!

Jonathan Livingston Seagull's creator tried to give up writing, but found himself finally compelled to write about the adventures of a "reluctant messiah." Richard Bach tells the story in the first person as his mentor, Donald Shimoda, schools him in the disciplines and wisdom of being a messiah. One of many surprises for Bach was that learning to do miracles is not the hard part about being a messiah. Walking on water comes relatively easy.

No, the greatest difficulty for Shimoda—himself a very experienced messiah—is that the crowds are only interested in the miracles. They do not care at all about anything he has to say. Shimoda laments: "It's not me they want, it's the miracles! And those I can teach to somebody else; let him be the Messiah. Miracles—like going to auto races to see the crashes—they came to me to see miracles. First it's frustrating and then after a while it just gets dull. I have no idea how the other messiahs could stand it."[5]

The purpose of the ministry is to point to the Word and to be in its service. The heroics of messiahship usually give the people what they want while distracting from the Word, which is itself the true miracle.

The proper care of the self for managing stress does not include messianic behavior that raises unrealistic expectations in parishioners. Certainly it will take a firm sense of self for a pastor to declare both by word and by deed that "I have no miracle to perform; rather, I have a ministry to work out with you as we serve Christ together." Also let it be clear that abdicating the role of messiah does not mean abdicating from the exercise of strong pastoral leadership. On the contrary, the possibility of exercising effective leadership is much enhanced when the pastor assertively enlists and organizes the congregation to carry out the church's ministry.

Finally, here are five areas of questioning that each pastor should consider in order to judge whether he or she is a candidate for the dubious distinction of messiah.

1. How much of your congregation's ministry and program fulfills their needs and is undergirded by lay leadership? After you are gone for one year, will the church's ministry be as strong or stronger than it is right now?

2. Could you without embarrassment explain your real goals and hopes for your congregation to three clergy colleagues? In other words, are the ambitions motivating you reasonable and realistic for one person to achieve with a congregation?

3. Could you also honestly discuss your own long-term personal and professional goals with three clergy friends? A pastor I knew collapsed in a worship service he was leading. A parishioner later said to him, "You are exhausted because you are trying to get a larger church!" My friend flatly denied it. Six months later he was telling this to a group of friends. After he had

finished, one of them quietly asked, "Why did you collapse from exhaustion?" My friend was silent. And then with honesty he admitted the truth he had been denying to himself, "Because I want a bigger church." There is nothing wrong with ambition, but would your ambitions, if they are truly realistic, stand the scrutiny of three of your colleagues?

4. How congruent is your "at home" personality with your "on the job" personality? How much of your humanness is present in your ministry? Are your pastoral relationships built on illusions about who you really are?

5. What price are you paying emotionally and physically for your ministry? Are you exhausting yourself trying to meet both your parishioners' and your own unrealistic expectations for your ministry?

The Scriptures speak of only one messiah, and probably that is all God needs. The ministry of the one Messiah will be the stronger as pastors care for themselves by offering their own persons, finiteness and all, in service for him. For it is in serving the Messiah, without trying to be a messiah, that the inevitable stress in ministry becomes manageable.

Untangling Responsibility

This Sunday morning was not much different from others. Pastor Gary Mason's Sunday routine always began at 5:45 A.M. He had his breakfast and made it to church by 6:45, just enough time for him to review his sermon once more and then prepare for the adult class he had to teach at 9:00 o'clock. But besides those responsibilities, he had to get ready for a special congregational meeting immediately following the 11:00 A.M. service. The district had given final approval for the addition to the Christian education building, and the congregation had to vote its approval. So there were a thousand details on Mason's mind. Also, there was to be a substitute organist this morning, and he had no idea how smoothly the service would go.

At the end of the adult class, just as he was gathering his papers, three class members descended upon him to find out his reaction to the recent denominational position paper on homosexuality. He felt trapped. He knew these people had him pegged as a liberal, and they wanted just one more piece of evidence to make their case against him. He had planned to preach on the sexuality issue, but that was to be in three months; he did not feel like discussing the matter this particular morning. Twelve minutes later he freed himself from the debate on homosexuality. Just as he slipped into his office the president of the church council handed him a file of papers that needed his signature before the congregational meeting.

"Details, details, details," he muttered to himself as he put his robe on and flung the stole around his neck. He glanced in the mirror to make sure he looked presentable, grabbed his sermon notes, and with a silent prayer on his lips strode toward the chancel door. Just as he put his hand to the knob, Sally Ferguson came rushing down the hall. "Pastor Mason, Pastor Mason," she whispered loudly. "I just heard from Claire Dancy that Ross Vander passed away last night. I suppose you have heard." Mechanically, Mason responded as he pulled the chancel door open, "No, I had not heard. Thank you, Sally."

Striding up the stairs into the chancel, he searched his memory. "Who is Ross Vander? Oh, yes, Betsy Vander was president of the deacons board eight or ten years ago, but has not been to church more than Easter and Christmas for the past five years. Old Ross has come to church only twice since I have been here. Now, let me see, the call to worship I was going to use was 'Let us worship and bow down, let us kneel . . .' " Mason took his seat behind the pulpit to wait for the substitute organist to finish the prelude. His final thoughts before standing for the call to worship were: "She's playing the organ much louder than Ruth usually does. A half dozen people will certainly complain after the service. But look at the attendance this morning. Not as many are on vacation as I had thought." The organ stopped, and Pastor Mason rose for the call to worship . . .

Tuesday morning the phone on Pastor Mason's desk rang at 9:01 A.M. "Hello, Pastor, this is Claire Dancy. I thought you might be interested to know I was just talking with Betsy Vander. They have asked the funeral home to locate another minister for Ross's funeral tomorrow." Mason's heart went to his throat as waves of guilt rushed over him. "Oh, no," he whispered as he set the phone down, "I completely forgot."

There is hardly a pastor with any experience who cannot remember a similar instance of serious professional oversight. It may not have been forgetting the death of a parishioner, but a similar situation that brought chagrin and humiliation. The weight of guilt reminds the pastor at a time like that: "I have blown it now! I am a failure."

On the surface, no one would excuse Pastor Mason for not contacting a family immediately upon learning of a death. That is a top priority for every pastor. Mason committed the unforgivable sin for pastors. On the other hand, he did receive the news at the worst possible time. He was entering the worship service, and also his mind was cluttered that morning with countless other details.

Pastor Mason's experience highlights a major issue for most clergy. The question is one of responsibility. It is the pastor's job to respond with integrity and leadership in meeting the various spiritual needs of the congregation and its members. For most clergy, their specific professional responsibilities are vaguely defined; nonetheless, they are a source of immense pressure. Hardly any other factor adds so much to the stress that a pastor has to manage week in and week out in the practice of ministry. One pastor summed it up as the number one issue today in the ministry: "That's our biggest fault in the ministry," he emphasized, "not deciding what is our responsibility and what is someone else's."

Among the chief manifestations of this problem are what James Glasse has labeled the conform/complaint and the bitch/brag syndromes that clergy easily fall into when two or three of them are gathered together.[6] The complaining typically blames the powers that be, whoever they are, from the bishop and the bureaucrats to the church secretary and the janitor. The whole congregation may also become a target of complaining. "If they only had the slightest sense of mission, they would recognize how seriously the neighborhood needs our attention as a church. But they are so blind to what the real mission of the church is!" This kind of complaining usually ends with the words, "If only . . ." "If only things were better or different, I could do my ministry the way it should be done."

Recovering potency for ministry. All pastoral responsibility rests upon the fact that the pastor is always in a position to make choices. There is no situation in which the pastor is not confronted with more than one option. Even though the Christian's power of choice may be limited to certain alternatives, the Christian is always in a position to make a response, to be "response-able." Indeed, all Christians are responsible for being the kind of persons they are, despite how much that appears to be out of their control. John Cobb explains Christian responsibility: "If I find that I am not a loving person, I must acknowledge my responsibility for not being a loving person; and if I find that I cannot even will to become a loving person, I must acknowledge responsibility for that failure of my will."[7] Whatever the set of circumstances, the Christian does not lose responsibility.

When clergy blame their situation on bishops, congregations, or secretaries, in effect they are saying that others, not they themselves, are responsible for them and their ministry. And by taking that attitude the pastor loses essential power and drifts, if not plummets, into impotency. Pastor Mason could have blamed many other people for the fact that he had not remembered Ross Vander's death. Most of all, he could have blamed the Vander family for remaining on the periphery of the congregation and not alerting him days or weeks earlier about Ross's declining health and the crisis that finally precipitated his death. Moreover, they could have called Mason immediately following Ross's death, which occurred on Saturday evening. But, they made no effort to get in touch with Mason. He received the news third-hand a day later.

As any pastor would understand, the experience for Mason was upsetting. He said later that it put his whole ministry into question that he had actually done such a thing. Yet in the midst of this critical personal and professional crisis, Pastor Mason affirmed his own basic responsibility that would not permit him to shift blame to anyone else.

> It is still churning around a bit, but it has not debilitated me. And I think the key to it was simply to be willing to take the responsibility. I am not blaming God, and I am not blaming the family, and I am not blaming the church.

By affirming his responsibility so clearly, Mason was freed to cope with the implications of his mistake and to initiate the action he needed to take toward the family.

Blaming would have immobilized him. He knew that himself:

> Pastors blame lay people, blame the church, and ultimately blame God. Rather than freeing a pastor, that limits a pastor's effectiveness, because personal power, personal potency is directly linked to personal responsibility. If you are not taking responsibility for who you are, then you are not going to be very powerful.

This same insight came to Pastor Rita Winters. After struggling through the depression that had gripped her for six months, she came to see that she was the only one with the power to change the conflict between herself and the senior pastor. Before she discovered her power, she had rendered herself helpless and had regarded herself as a victim. As a victim, she found depression was her only possible response because she had given her own power over to the senior pastor, the church, and the bishop. She could look back and see clearly what had happened.

> Taking responsibility for self was something that I was totally unprepared to do two years ago. I found myself in a bad situation and blaming it on the church, the senior pastor, the hierarchy. Why didn't somebody do something about this? I think it took me a long time to realize that I could do something, that I didn't have to be a pawn in the situation.

All responsibility for a pastor's ministry must rest finally upon the pastor. One finds strength for self by being responsible in whatever situation one finds oneself. Without the power inherent in that responsibility there will be no management of stress.

Counterfeits for responsibility.   Accepting full responsibility for oneself offers a dimension of freedom that is unique to the Christian faith. However, too many clergy do not experience freedom in their ministry because they do not function out of responsibility but out of obligation, or inflated self-importance, or dread that someone may not like them. Though these three negative motivations for ministry sound different, they may be three aspects of the same dynamic. Certainly they all readily pass among many clergy as counterfeits for the responsibility that effectively deals with stress.

Pastor Robert Horton is now serving a respectable suburban congregation, and he is affirmed with respect by his colleagues. Ministry is not nearly as difficult for him as it once was. By his own acknowledgment, he did not handle stress at all well for the first several years he was in the parish. The lesson he had to learn related to the counterfeits for responsibility. Somehow he had received the notion when he was ordained that his purpose as a minister was to ensure that all members of his congregation were happy all the time. Since they were not happy all the time, it could only be one person's fault—the pastor's. Needless to say, such an assignment kept Horton busy. For a while he was up to it. It took him too long to figure out that there is another purpose for ministry than keeping everybody happy. "If something went wrong in the parish I somehow felt this tremendous need to try to apologize to people, or make sure they were O.K. I was afraid that if I did something wrong someone might be terribly upset."

Pastor John Ziegler, on the other hand, feels guilty when he does not obey the counterfeits for responsibility. His whole ministry is based on his need to belong to everyone else in his world and not to belong to himself. He has given away all his power by obligating himself to all his parishioners. He explains: "If I feel I need an afternoon off or a day off, I question if I really need that because other people don't get the time off they want either." He says yes to all demands on his time because "If I do say no, I feel guilty. I am there to serve people, so anyone who wants help should be able to come to me, and I should always be ready, willing, and able to give that help." The final test for Ziegler is how his popularity rating reads. Anything less than one hundred percent spells disaster: "If I am serving, then I am best as a servant if I am liked by everybody."

A pastor who is prepared to function as a responsible decision maker will be able to discern the alternatives and choose the options whereby ministry can best be served. But the pastor who has confused choice-making with obligation has surrendered both personal and professional integrity. That pastor is at the mercy of whoever wants to put the next claim on his or her time.

In the face of such capitulation, the possibilities for being swamped by stress are countless. Pastor Shirley Johnson reflected an element of truth when she observed: "I think the church has limitless expectations of the pastor. Unless you have seen everybody three times in a month plus done all the other things, you have never really accomplished the task. It's always an open-ended job. You never get it done. You never can." But she also reflected more truth when she commented on herself and other pastors who complain about the obligations they have: "I think we do blame committees for scheduling things that we feel forced to attend, and feel as though we have no control over it. Actually we have total control if we want to exert it. I think we cave in because of the desire to always look good." Johnson also noted that the pressure often comes from within the pastor. "I put the expectation that I should attend a meeting on my parishioners rather than recognizing that it is my own expectation of what I think I ought to be doing. If I were not at a meeting and had a good reason for not being there, it would be acceptable. People are much more lenient and generous than we pastors suspect they will be."

Limit-setting.   There cannot be responsibility without saying no. For the self to claim its own power of choice-making, there is no way to avoid setting limits. Responsibility requires making choices about commitments and setting priorities to values. The choice for one option is always a choice against other alternatives. Pastoral ministry invariably involves choices where no has to be said.

Pastor Larry Ferguson related a recent experience. About 10:30 P.M. on a Saturday night, a woman in his congregation called Ferguson on the phone and said that she was so upset about her marriage she had to talk with him right then. So she came over to the parsonage, and drank coffee and reviewed her domestic problems until 3:30 A.M. Ferguson tried to explain: "I find it more difficult to say no to people in the church. It is the bugaboo of saying no to your employer. It would have been hard for me to say to her, 'I have to get up early in the morning. I'm going to have to ask you to leave.' "

Obviously Pastor Ferguson failed to make the important distinction between his own self-care and what he imagines to be the expectations of his parishioners. He is not functioning as a free and responsible pastor, but as one that is ready to *be* whatever his parishioners say they want him to be. He is particularly vulnerable in the area of offering help. Whatever kind of help his parishioners think they need, Ferguson surrenders. His purpose as a pastor is not determined within himself but by the expressed need of his parishioner, even at 3:30 A.M. He has no limits as a helper. How disillusioning that helping process must be, both for himself and for those whom presumably he is helping!

Responsibility for parish ministry.   It is not possible to manage the pressures in ministry without a clear understanding of pastoral responsibility. The first step for the pastor is always to make the careful distinction between one's personal identity and one's human failings. Pastor

Gary Mason could not have coped with his forgetting the death of Ross Vander if he had identified himself with that error and concluded that he himself was a failure as a person. He had failed in an important pastoral responsibility, but he was not himself a failure. Secondly, it is equally important for the pastor not to identify with the failures and inadequacies others attribute to the pastor. There is a very important distinction in the statement, "I am not incompetent as a self, but my professional performance as a pastor may well be judged inadequate in certain areas." Indeed, if as a pastor you find that your professional competence is inadequate, you will be in a better position to deal with that fact if your sense of selfhood is still intact.

The third necessary step for pastors who would keep their sense of responsibility untangled is to discover and negotiate a realistic job description. Too many pastors have little or no sense of priorities for their ministry. In their minds everything holds nearly equal importance. Today we will do youth work, tomorrow we write the newsletter, and the next day we call on the shut-ins. When a pastor considers everything in the church's program to be of equal importance, it means that he or she must try to be involved in everything.

The problem with this approach is that many pastors obligate themselves to do more than their parishioners really think is necessary. Wise pastors sit down and negotiate with their pastor-parish relations committee or their personnel committee about the priorities for their congregation's ministry. The pastor's strengths, expertise, and interests are taken into account. The lay leaders also identify the major needs that they see in the church. Then both the pastor and the lay leaders can negotiate where the pastor's energies will be directed, with the understanding that the areas of lower priority will not receive very much if any of the pastor's attention.

One pastor explained the results from negotiating with his pastor-parish relations committee: "I like to do youth work, and our youth program is sagging now. But the committee and I both feel membership evangelism is a higher priority. So for the next six months I will not even touch the youth program." That left the pastor free to say: "I don't take all the blame or all the credit. It is a mutual ministry, and that is the corner of my ecclesiology." And it can only be a mutual ministry because the priorities are clear for the congregation and for the pastor. Effective limits for ministry have thus been recognized, benefiting both the pastor and the church's ministry.

The fourth necessary step for clarifying responsibility is for the pastor to learn to distinguish between minor and major crises. Except for the death of a parishioner, it is hard to imagine any pastoral counseling that must occur after 11:00 P.M. and before 9:00 A.M. Even those threatening suicide can be told that they are indeed loved and cared for, and that both they and their pastor will have clearer minds for sorting through their despair at 9:00 A.M. than at 4:30 A.M.

Finally, there are three tests you can use to determine how well you have straightened out your own understanding of pastoral responsibility. The first is the telephone test. When the phone rings does your heart start pounding as you wonder what emergency is about to land in your lap? The second is the "no" test. It is simple. Can you pronounce that word to a parishioner? The third is the guilt test. Is guilt one of the major motivating forces in your ministry? If you consistently fail any of these three tests, you will do well to examine carefully your presuppositions about ministry. The data would suggest that your understanding of responsibility still needs refining for effective stress management.

CHAPTER 5

Coping with Time, Anger, and Conflict

Time, like an ever-rolling stream,
  Bears all its sons away;
They fly forgotten, as a dream
  Dies at the opening day.
      (The Worshipbook) [1]

For everything there is a season, and a time
for every matter under heaven:
  a time to be born, and a time to die;
  a time to plant, and a time to pluck up what is
    planted;
  a time to kill, and a time to heal;
  a time to break down, and a time to build up.
      (Ecclesiastes 3:1–3)

Managing stress for the sake of ministry cannot be done adequately if a pastor is trying to perform at extraordinary levels, or if the pastor does not have a realistic perspective about professional responsibility. Effective self-care in the ministry also calls for decisions regarding one's use of time, one's expression of anger, and one's response to interpersonal conflict. The issues of time, anger, and conflict cannot be avoided if the pressures in ministry are to be handled satisfactorily.

Putting Everything in Its Proper Time

Responsible persons manage time instead of allowing time to manage them. Certainly time has its inevitabilities, but time does not dictate how those inevitabilities must be regarded. All things have their seasons, and it is wise to accept what is beyond our control. However, many elements of time are within our control, and we can manage their place within the structure we give to our own time. The pastor who fails to plan will become a victim, for people and events can readily impose their own structure upon the pastor's time.[2]

It is no surprise to hear that a pastor who has lost control of time has also lost important aspects of personal identity. Pastor Tom Abrams recalls the period in his ministry when, as a senior pastor and rising star in his conference, he was working eighty hours a week.

> I tried to remold that congregation in a certain form, and lost contact with who I was myself. I took on different attributes in that particular time. I became much more rigid, lost a lot of ability to compromise, lost an ability to relate easily with other people without carrying agendas into the situation. I became more of an authoritarian figure than I had been prior to that.

Who can say if there is a cause-and-effect relationship between working eighty hours a week and undergoing such a dramatic shift in one's personal identity? But when the self loses its own center and its own power to choose, it capitulates to stress. The self becomes vulnerable to forces pulling it aimlessly in countless directions at once. A primary symptom of such a loss of identity is the loss of control over one's time.

Pastor Sharon Barker comments on her own experience in managing time. Earlier she had been depressed about the demands made upon her by her ministry.

> I now see clearly the need to be disciplined about how you carry out your life. The time that you need for yourself does not just happen. You cannot just count on it being left over at the end of the week. For me, this discovery involved getting more control over my own day, my own schedule, what I am doing with my life. I get up and I know I am going to have an hour in the morning that I can use for exercise and for meditation before I leave the house, and I need that. I know that I am going to have certain time to spend with friends, certain time for family. Those things have to be worked out or they will not happen. If I did not make those definite plans, my schedule would end up running me, and I would be back where I started, depressed and not coping.

Many pastors report similar discoveries in their own lives. A firm grasp on their own power as centered persons requires a firm grasp on the structure of their own time and their commitments for that time.

A sacred idea that needs reconsideration.   The single "day off" per week is the yardstick by which clergy supposedly measure their commitment to ministry and their allotted time for leisure and relaxation. It is commonplace to hear pastors say which day is their day off. Invariably, they add that recently they have not been taking their day off because there just has not been time.

Who knows where the notion of the pastor's one day off got started? It can hardly be demonstrated that such an idea is biblical. Maybe the thought of a pastor taking only one day a week away from ministerial duties had its origin in rural settings where the parishioners typically worked in their fields six days a week.[3] If parishioners work such long hours, certainly the pastor should work just as long.

The time has come to reexamine that "one day off"

idea. First of all, most pastors do in fact take more time away from their pastoral duties than just one day a week. Furthermore, it is a form of spiritual arrogance for pastors to suggest to parishioners, who work only a four- or five-day week, that the pastor's work requires six days a week. A wise layperson will not be fooled, but rather will ask some questions: "Does my pastor really work six days a week? If so, why? Is there something wrong with my pastor? Isn't the pastor shortchanging some part of his or her life by working so many hours for the church? Is that what Christian dedication is supposed to mean, the sacrifice of family and marriage?" We pastors do well to listen to such questioning!

Far more important issues for time management. For pastors to gain effective control of their own time, at least seven issues need to be considered. First of all, there is the issue of work habits. There are only 168 hours in each week, and Sunday comes around once every seven days. Some have thought that by giving up eating, sleeping, and family life they could lengthen their week. Not so. There is no trick by which you can add one cubit to your stature or one hour to your week. Pastors must live and work within the limitations of a twenty-four-hour day. But that is difficult for many. After studying the work habits of a group of pastors, time management consultants Merrill Douglass and Joyce McNally came to "the inescapable conclusion . . . that the ministers spent most of their time doing the least important things."[4] Their time was wasted by:

1. Interruptions, telephone calls, drop-in visitors, distractions
2. Leaving tasks unfinished, jumping from one thing to another
3. Doing routine tasks, [getting] involved in too much trivia

4. Attempting too much at once, [making] unrealistic time estimates
5. Cluttered desk and office, personal disorganization[5]

The second important issue is priorities. How clearly focused are your priorities for ministry? A pastor should be able to write down five or six major priorities that can be translated into plans for specific ministry activities during the week. An example: Hospital calling is a high priority. The specific activity plan is that every Tuesday and Friday morning I will drive to both the hospitals in town to see my parishioners. Another example: Preaching is a high priority. The specific activity plan is that Monday, Wednesday, and Thursday mornings are absolutely set aside for preparation of the sermon without any interruptions except the rare emergency.

Once you have listed your priorities for your ministry on paper, ask whether your lay leadership would agree with your list. Your priorities should be negotiated, mutually agreed upon by your lay leaders and you. If they are not, your efforts will be scattered because you will be trying to satisfy, to some extent, two sets of priorities for your time. You will be trying to meet the expectations of your board as well as trying to meet your own priorities for ministry. That is a perfect setup for a tension headache.

Are your priorities vague and general, or are they specific? Are they specific enough so that they must be renegotiated periodically? Maybe youth ministry is a high priority in the fall, but by spring you and your board may wish to reconsider and put youth ministry lower down, or even drop it from your list of priorities. If your priorities are not clear, as they are not for many clergy, you will be like a base runner trying to touch all the bases at the same time. Of course it cannot be done, but you can certainly exhaust yourself trying!

The third issue for every pastor to examine is the effectiveness of time use. Pastor Nordquist works forty hours a week between Monday and Saturday. His time on Sunday is beyond those forty hours, depending on his particular responsibilities each Sunday. He is the pastor of a downtown church of more than six hundred members. There were two pastors at the church before he came to serve the church by himself. He plans his time carefully, so from one hour to the next he knows what he will be doing, with room for some flexibility in his schedule. He explains, "In the eight hours that I work in a day, I now get more done. I do less daydreaming and less sitting around because on my schedule at 9:00 o'clock on Monday morning it says that it is sermon preparation time. So administration stops and sermon writing starts at 9:00 o'clock."

Many pastors put in long hours because they take two or three hours to do what could have been done in half the time. If a pastor's hospital visits generally last over a half hour, and if counseling sessions with parishioners last over one and a half hours, then that pastor needs to begin using time for pastoral care more efficiently!

The fourth issue is accountability. The parish ministry is not to be thought of as a private practice or one's own personal enterprise. Pastors are accountable to their boards and to their parishioners. Like it or not, the pastor is employed by the congregation and (in most instances) paid by the congregation. If a pastor forgets that fact, some astute layperson will surely see that the pastor is reminded of it. How a pastor uses time is a matter of proper concern to the congregation and its officers. One pastor has rightly observed that such accountability is integral to the parish ministry:

> Congregations are beginning to demand of ministers at least a minimal level of efficiency and accountability in

areas that can be open to scrutiny. That demand should not be seen as distrust so much as concern for the ministry and its accomplishment of the mission of the church. That mission, and ultimately the ministry of the church, is the responsibility of every Christian.[6]

As a pastor makes plans, it is important to demonstrate a responsible stewardship of time. Some pastors validate their accountability by turning in once a month a tally sheet of how many hours they have worked, how many hospital calls they have made, and how many home communions they have served, etc. Others simply demonstrate their accountability by telling the congregation that certain hours will be reserved for office work, and the pastor will usually be found in the office at those announced times.

A pastor is wise to negotiate the priorities for ministry with the church board or council, and then once every six months to review performance in the light of those specific, measurable goals. This type of review can be relatively nonthreatening, and can help both the pastor and laypersons to understand better how effectively pastoral time is being used. Such a periodic review is desirable because it looks at the question of effectiveness more comprehensively than is possible by a monthly tally sheet showing the number of hospital calls made.[7]

The fifth issue to be considered for effective time management is balance. Despite the number of hours a person works during the week, there are basic needs that must be satisfied in that person's life. A pastor should ask how well personal needs for exercise, meditation, leisure, recreation, and time with spouse or family are being met. One pastor said: "I was an early proponent of 'It's not the quantity of time spent with one's family that is important, it's the quality.' I did a hundred variations on that for quite a while. I have since decided that

that was pure rationalization. For me, the quantity of time is important!"

Part of the question of balance in one's schedule has to do with one's interests. Are you using your time in such a way as to capitalize on your interests? At least two thirds of your time should be used for activities that truly interest you. If you are not basically doing what satisfies your interests, your efficiency and productivity will begin to diminish.

To achieve balance in the use of time, you need to consider your work pattern and work rhythm. Do you work ahead of deadlines, or do you wait until the last minute and work best under pressure? Do you need several mornings to prepare a sermon, or do you prefer to sit in front of the typewriter for one long stretch until it is completed? Respecting your most efficient work pattern is essential for productive time management.

The sixth issue, and a critical one, is the need to limit outside community and judicatory commitments. A pastor can feel quite important and useful when asked to serve on various community boards and committees. But invariably, exhausted pastors can point to their extracurricular activities as a principal source of stress in their overcrowded calendars. Excessive outside commitments are the first place many pastors realize they need to cut back if they are to get their schedule and their life back under control.

The seventh and final issue is dealing with criticism. Are you working hard all the time in order to avoid criticism? A pastor must accept the fact that not everyone will like everything that is done, and that criticism cannot be entirely avoided. Criticism should be expected; it should be evaluated, and some of it disregarded. Once one has learned that criticism is inevitable, and that it does not mean the end of one's ministry, then one can take hold of the day and shape it so as to meet one's priorities and not simply to satisfy one's imagined critics.

The modular framework. The modular approach to time management is one method that is becoming increasingly popular among pastors. The advantage of this method is that it recognizes that most tasks undertaken by a pastor require blocks of time made up of several hours, not just one or two hours. Hospital calling may take an entire afternoon; administration may well require a full morning in the office. A pastor generally spends more than one hour at a time working on a sermon.

A module is a unit of time composed of three to four hours. In each waking day there are three modules: morning, afternoon, and evening. Thus in a seven-day week there are twenty-one modules.

A pastor decides how many of those twenty-one modules will be given to work for the parish. Let us say that you have designated thirteen for ministry.[8] On a sheet of paper block out your work schedule for those thirteen modules. As you do that, recognize that if you work three modules in one day, you can justify taking only one or two modules for work the next day. Also keep in mind that you will probably work an extra module in the week just responding to crises and unanticipated emergencies.

An important advantage to the modular system is that it sets limits to a pastor's work periods. Many pastors take home extra stress because they are not sure when they are working or when they can call their time their own. Psychologically we function best when we can set limits to our work periods and delineate clearly between work and personal or private time. An additional advantage to the modular system is that the pastor's family knows when the pastor will be available for family commitments and relationships. Posting the weekly modular schedule on the refrigerator door can be an effective way to demonstrate to the family that the pastor intends to stay within limits for work at the church.

The pastor who bases ministry on good self-care will manage the day so that almost everything falls into its proper perspective. For example, Pastor Gordon Ellingson finally reached a balance in his ministry by learning to manage his time more effectively. He even goes to a health spa two or three times a week, which years ago he would have felt guilty doing. He also permits himself to spend more relaxed time with his wife.

> Now I am able to stop working at three in the afternoon if I have a meeting at night, and be home when my wife comes home from work at 3:30. I sit down and drink coffee with her and spend a couple of hours just talking with her or doing something with my son. I couldn't have done that a couple of years ago, or if I had done it I would have felt guilty about doing it. In fact, I think now that the quality of my ministry improves as the quantity of time I give to it decreases!

Everything has its time. When ministry gets the time it deserves, and no more, all will be done as well as it is going to be done. Lloyd Rediger has drawn the proper conclusion:

> Time is a gift from God. But time has limits and so do we. The sense of time-urgency tells us when we are struggling with God's gift and the limits of it. It also indicates an opportunity for growth in our lives.[9]

Anger, Conflict, and Stress Management

It is 10:52 P.M. Pastor Carl Peterson speaks to the church council after a long evening and following a close vote on a decisive issue.

> Let me make an observation about what is going on here. I am angry about what was said on the decision that has

just been made. I want to share that with you because that is really how I feel. I sense that some of you feel the same way. Now, how are we going to be honest with those feelings? Can we put them out there on the table, and then do something constructive and something positive about this issue? That will not be easy because I would just like to yell like hell at all of you right now, but that is not going to be helpful.

Conflict cannot be avoided in parish ministry. Pastors cannot avoid feeling angry at times with their parishioners and with their councils or boards. Anger is a part of ministry and an inevitable fact of life in any congregation. In his helpful book on conflict resolution, Alan Filley describes the basic characteristics of a conflict situation, dynamics that occur in many congregations.

1. At least two parties (individuals or groups) are involved in some kind of interaction.
2. Mutually exclusive goals and/or mutually exclusive values exist, in fact or as perceived by the parties involved.
3. Interaction is characterized by behavior designed to defeat, reduce, or suppress the opponent or to gain a mutually designated victory.
4. The parties face each other with mutually opposing actions and counteractions.
5. Each party attempts to create an imbalance or a relatively favored position of power vis-à-vis the other.[10]

Probably no other emotion is more threatening to experience than one's own rage. Instinctively we know that within our own personality is an immense force that can be exceedingly destructive if it should ever get loose from our control. Anxiety about our rage is mainly due to the fear that we might lose control of our rage. Losing control is such a terrifying prospect that many persons tightly control their anger lest their rage leap from their rational restraint.

The issue for the pastor is how to function in an environment that is sometimes hostile (yes, even in the church) while maintaining a firm sense of one's integrity. Part of the task for the pastor is to acknowledge one's own anger when it occurs without becoming identified with it. Having recognized the reality of one's anger, the pastor must decide how best to express it, making that decision out of a spirit that values love for others. This is no small task. If there is a single, common professional crisis that all pastors confront, it is most certainly the crisis of deciding how they shall handle their anger. Decisions of how at various times to express anger will reflect a pastor's deepest personal and spiritual values.

Commonly reported issues.   As pastors talk about how they have dealt with conflicts in their congregation or with conflicts between themselves and parishioners, certain common themes begin to emerge. The most frequent issue with which most pastors have to cope within themselves is their fear of rejection because they have allowed their anger to be expressed. Not all pastors identify this as a fear of rejection, but as a concern that parishioners will not respect them if their anger is revealed. One pastor linked this fear within himself to an experience he had when he was a child. He had become angry with another child, and that child responded by pushing him into a mud puddle. His shoes, socks, and trousers were dirty, and the experience was humiliating. Now when he anticipates the possibility of conflict between himself and a parishioner, he remembers that incident. "I'm afraid that if I really get angry at somebody, that person will get angry at me. And if that happens, I am in big trouble." Intellectually he realizes that conflict is inevitable in the church; still his emotional reaction, from deep within, remains: "I do not need to be liked by everybody, but I do not like to be disliked by anybody." Another experienced pastor acknowledged the difficulty he had had over the years in these words: "My risk always was, are they still going to like me? Are they still going to like me if I reveal that side of me, my angry, upset side?"

A second, commonly held assumption is that being angry or expressing anger does not fit one's image of a "good" pastor. Pastor William Rogers knew that he was getting angry with the attitudes of some of his church officers, but he told himself to ignore those feelings and to pretend that they would go away. It just did not seem right to him as a pastor to be angry with his church officers. But despite his efforts to ignore his feelings, his family was receiving the brunt of the anger that he carried home from the church.

> I was making a clear distinction between me as pastor and me as person, which as I look back now was a pretty stupid thing to do. I sat on a hell of a lot of anger for a long time. I would come home and "beat the wife, kick the kid, and throw out the dog." All of which was really a denial or a suppression of me as a person. I began to think after awhile, "Gee, that's not too genuine. Not very honest either." Then I began to get in touch with that anger again.

A pastor's self-image has a strong effect upon how one tries to cope with stressful situations. Another pastor put it in these words, something of an insight for him and a matter of frustration: "I realized, especially in retrospect, I do not have the freedom to be angry directly with people." One can almost hear another vow being added to the ordination service: "Do you promise that, from now on, none of your parishioners will ever hear or see a trace of your anger—only your family will? If so, say 'I promise.'"

Many pastors feel uncomfortable expressing their anger because they have been hurt by a dominating authority figure such as a parent, teacher, or pastor. Consequently they have resolved that they will never be like that person and will never do to others what was done to them. In fact, one of their motivations for ministry is often to demonstrate the caring, understanding, and gentle qualities that they never experienced from that authority figure.

In other words, they have adopted a model for ministry that is never to include the expression of anger or forcefulness. Usually, when such a decision is made, the resolve is so strong that there is an overcompensation as the pastor adopts a passive approach to pastoral leadership. When such pastors show the slightest bit of assertiveness, they feel as if they are becoming a dictator. In effect, such persons lose the ability to make a realistic judgment about the strength of their own anger. A whisper to such a person can sound like a roar. As a result, much anger is denied, and a consistently passive response is given to most parish crises. Many parishioners may wonder why their pastor never takes a strong stand, and meanwhile the pastor's own assessment is that he or she is just a hair's breadth from becoming a tyrant. Seward Hiltner makes an observation about such pastors when he says:

> Today, I think, too many ministers settle for too little power. Some kind of power is needed if service is to be performed. This ought not to be "power over," in the sense of overriding anybody without consulting him seriously. But the retreat to "just doing my job" violates the whole conception of ministry.[11]

Another factor that immobilizes many pastors in the midst of conflict is their naiveté, their lack of political sense for the deeper meanings and interactions that go on behind the scenes. It is characteristic of such pastors to take at face value what all the people say. They trust everyone explicitly. Door-to-door salesmen love to find them at home. Used-car salesmen make their living off such trusting souls. The warning signals of conflict go past such pastors completely unnoticed. Next a tornado of conflict is camped on their doorstep, and they have not the slightest idea what has caused it. Such outright naiveté is not an asset for effective conflict resolution in the parish.

The messiah of the sponge.   Pastor Patrick Bloomquist came to a large suburban congregation that had several factions in it which seemed always to be at odds. The divisions in the church were draining off everyone's energy, and the church's mission was being left by the wayside. For three or four years, Bloomquist proceeded on the assumption that his best pastoral strategy was to be the great listener. He was going to be the sounding board or the dart board whenever anyone was angry, whether they were angry with someone else or with him. He simply accepted their anger and conveyed total understanding. However, he learned that such passive acceptance of anger, even if it was not all personal, can soon exact a heavy emotional toll. Bloomquist's strategy nearly marked the end of his ministry because he soon found his own emotional resources exhausted. He recalled the experience this way:

> I did something which was rather destructive to me. I became a sponge at one point in my relationship with the parish. I noticed that there were so many conflicts going on I adopted the pattern of permitting anybody who had a conflict to dump it on me. So I became a great masochist, soaking up all the conflict in the parish, soaking it up, and soaking it up.
>
> That works! The church had a chance to vent its feelings. The leaders had a chance to say where they stood. It does build stronger community. But, man, it destroyed me! At the end of four years I was really beaten down. I realized then that I was not taking care of myself. I was

literally destroying myself. I was the messiah of the sponge—my symbol. [I was] the disciple of the sponge, the apostle of the sponge. I had on my shield a great big sponge, just like St. Peter has the keys. My role was to absorb everything!

The messiah of the sponge reformed. Pastor Bloomquist decided that there had to be a more effective way to take care of himself and to exercise pastoral leadership for handling conflict. He still listens to those who need to express their anger. But then he either lets them know how he feels about what they have just said, or he directs them to the proper committee or person in the church who can help them with their concern.

First of all I let a person sound off. I still do that. But when they are finished, I clarify for them where they need to go with their feelings. If [their anger] is with me, I say, "I'm sorry you feel that way." And then I explain where I stand. But if it deals with someone else in the church, I say, "I think that you had better go and share that information with the other person." That way I wrap it up and turn it around. I may also say to them, "That's pretty heavy stuff you're dropping on me. I really don't like that." So I let them know how I feel.

Bloomquist follows this stance of openness and directness also with his church board. On one occasion he made his position clear ahead of time, namely, that the congregation should take the initiative in relating directly to the community around the church. When the church officers turned down a proposed program for community outreach, he expressed his anger and his disappointment over the decision. In this way he and his church officers maintain open communication so they may clearly understand whether or not they are sharing in a ministry of mutual goals and purposes.

Pastors who are coping with anger and conflict. Each pastor will develop a personal style for relating to persons with whom there is a conflict. Three basic considerations appropriately concern a pastor when conflict arises. Regarding the individual or individuals directly in conflict with the pastor, what constitutes pastoral care for those persons who are expressing both hurt and anger? Do those persons need understanding only, or understanding plus confrontation, or simply some explanation in order to satisfy questions and concerns? How can their anger be clarified so they may understand the issues lying behind it? These are important pastoral care questions that should concern the pastor when dealing with persons who are reacting angrily.

Another important consideration relates to the overall welfare of the congregation. A pastor needs to take into account the impact of divisive issues upon the life of a congregation. What is the best way to handle a conflict if a dozen prominent families who make up one third of the leadership of the congregation threaten to leave the church if certain of the pastor's mission policies are carried out?[12] The peace and unity of the church is an appropriate concern of the pastor in formulating strategy for handling conflict. Speed Leas and Paul Kittlaus, writing on this subject, speak to other difficulties that may arise if a pastor decides that conflict in the congregation must be kept behind the scenes:

> It is not possible for anyone to control or to stop a conflict. It may be possible by one ploy or another to inhibit it temporarily. But to put chains on it at one moment is surely to guarantee that it will break those chains at some time in the future.
>
> The cost of conflict avoided or repressed is usually greater than the cost of conflict faced and dealt with. The lingering agony of the unresolved concerns, the energy that is sapped in containing feelings or denying needs, and the clever games that must be played in order to keep the organization barely alive are rarely worth the short-

term pain of coping with difference. However, in some rare situations, where the costs may be higher than the risk of repressing the conflict (as in the case of the great likelihood of violence), repression may be an appropriate strategy.[13]

A third and equally important consideration is what the pastor needs to do to care for himself or herself. "How vulnerable am I willing to become?" is an essential question. Moreover, it should also be asked: "How much emotional strain and stress can I carry? Do I preserve the unity of the church at the cost of the disintegration of myself and my family? If I am not to disintegrate, literally fall to pieces, where must I draw the lines and declare my boundaries? How can I remain centered within my own integrity, not becoming overly identified with personalities and issues that can easily distort my perspective on myself and my loving perspective toward others and the church?" These are all basic questions that a pastor should weigh carefully in order to practice appropriate self-care, pastoral care for angry and hurting persons, and the care of the church as a whole.

Each pastor must make that private choice when the moment of decision is at hand. When Pastor Glen Andrews and his wife were called to old First Church, they were told that the trustees were about to approve the building of a new parsonage. However, after the Andrews family arrived, it soon became apparent that the call committee had made a rash promise. The trustees were still trying to make up their minds. Meanwhile, the new pastor and his family lived in the old parsonage. They especially tried to be patient about the heating system, which like the rest of the house was terribly inadequate and produced a fine soot that the family breathed every hour they were at home.

Pastor Andrews went to the next trustees meeting with much anticipation because he knew the issue of the new parsonage was to be decided. After much inconclusive debate and foot-dragging, someone proposed that the matter be tabled until the next meeting. Promptly Pastor Andrews rose to his feet and left the meeting. He ran next door to the parsonage and strode determinedly through the front door into the living room. He later recalled that his wife "was sitting there, wondering what this whirlwind was that came flying in the door."

He yanked the register out of the floor and grabbed the piece of filter material that was "filthy black." He took it into the kitchen and wrapped the dirty filter in Saran Wrap so he would not lose any of the soot. Then he ran back over to the church. He took his coat off and felt his heart beating wildly because he was so enraged.

He took a deep breath, and then very purposefully he walked back into the trustees meeting. There was an awesome silence in the room. He laid the black filter material in the middle of the table saying, "While you people are deciding to postpone this issue for another month, my family and I are breathing that crap!"

In his own words Andrews related that experience:

> I could hardly talk. My throat was tight, my jaw would not move. My tongue would not work. I was almost paralyzed by my anger. But I got it out, and I said, "I do not care whether you build a new manse or whether you do not build a new manse, but I wish you would decide. It really does not matter to me. But if you do not want to build a new manse, then please say so, so we can talk about a housing allowance."

Besides matters of housing, the annual salary review may be an important time for a pastor to risk conflict by clearly stating financial needs. Pastor Charles Hawkins was in a church that decided not to hire another pastor after his colleague resigned. So Hawkins was left to carry the additional workload. He agreed to the revised job description, but he was infuriated when the church council recommended only a $900 salary raise. "I got very angry at first," he recalled. "Then I went back to the church council and presented my case for a greater raise because I was assuming the full pastoral leadership of the church. The result was that the council reconsidered its previous action and decided upon a $1,700 raise instead."

The energy from one's anger can help a pastor to deal directly with vital issues such as salary. That is why Pastor Phil Arndt gets right to the point about his annual salary increase:

> I realize that when I sit down with the finance committee to talk about my contract for next year they are not going to suggest a satisfactory increase unless I say something. They suggested a one-percent increase over the cost of living raise, and I said, "No, I believe it should be three percent over the cost of living raise." And they agreed. No one is going to take care of you unless you take care of yourself.

Maintaining selfhood invariably requires self-definition which explains where one's limits are. Some pastors would like to think that if they have no clear limits and boundaries, they can merge flexibly with any situation and any personalities. However, this is a misunderstanding of Paul's statement, "I have become all things to all men" (I Cor. 9:22). Failure to define sufficiently one's needs and interests is usually a preliminary factor in causing circumstances to escalate to conflict. Pastors who effectively cope with conflict have consistently found it necessary somehow to define their interests, needs, and the limits to what they will do in their ministry.

Pastor John Weber has come to feel increasingly more comfortable about stating his limits to his parishioners. One example occurred when his council was discussing having Sunday evening services. He said that he would not assume the full responsibility for the services. He explained that he wanted a group of laypersons to assume that responsibility and to do the planning. He also said that he would not follow the same format every Sunday evening of reading Scripture and preaching a sermon. With those limitations, however, he was certainly willing to work with whatever plan the committee would formulate. On another occasion, in a trustees meeting, he said he would not be responsible to lock and unlock the church restrooms on Sundays. That, he felt, should be anyone else's responsibility but his, and he made that point clear for all to understand.

Pastor Ray Fortner drew a limit when a couple he was visiting complained that they found it hard to listen to his sermons because of the way he stroked his beard while he preached. Fortner replied to them: "Listen, do not tell me about that. You can tell me about a lot of things that disturb you about the church and our worship service, but when you start talking about my stroking my beard, that is an idiosyncrasy. You have your idiosyncrasies and I have mine!"

If a pastor never sets limits in relationships with parishioners or colleagues, that pastor is not practicing the self-care that is necessary for ministry. Otherwise, as Fortner pointed out, "If I do not affirm myself and what I deem to be important, I am a target for anyone who would make me into their own." Clearly, a pastor cannot be faithful in ministry without having recognizable limits and boundaries.

Finally, most experienced pastors who deal with conflict in a straightforward manner speak positively of the benefits that come from facing openly the painful issues. One pastor tries to use conflict as an opportunity for educating the congregation. He asks the people to celebrate their diversity and to see their conflict as a source of learning and as a laboratory for sharing honest differences. Another pastor reports that it has been valuable for people to see that he gets angry just as they do.

> It makes me seem more human. I think people see me as
> more of a human being. Sometimes I have actually said,
> "I am a human being and you cannot say, and you cannot
> do, things like this without my feeling it."

His other positive benefit was to discover that his parishioners do not feel badly that he "loses his cool." When he has expressed his anger he has received comments such as "Well, the minister lost his cool tonight," or "Gee, I am glad you did it. Somebody else should have done it earlier!"

Pastors who have learned to cope with their own anger generally affirm the importance of being open and communicating clearly about their feelings. In the long run, the parishioners respond positively because they find their pastor to be a person who can be trusted in the midst of conflict. The lay people as a rule can be trusted also, as Pastor Gene Gilson notes:

> There are a few who trick you and deceive you, but not
> all two hundred fifty of them; not all persons in the
> church are that way. There are always some people who
> are supportive. I think that too often pastors go into a
> congregation and create situations, or do not share
> enough of themselves because they worry about what
> other people are going to think of them. So they end
> up putting themselves on a pedestal because the people
> like them on the pedestal, and they do not bother to
> share who they really are. That is what causes disruptions.

Every pastor's style of leadership needs periodic examination. Many difficulties in handling conflict may be of the pastor's making! The constructive alternative for the pastoral use of assertiveness has been succinctly outlined by Augsburger:

> Assertiveness as a lifestyle involves certain convictions,
> certain affirmations:
> "I have equal worth with others. I can affirm the mutual

worth of both self and others. I am worthful."

"I have equal rights with others. I will assert my wants while affirming your equal rights. I will prize justice."

"I am confident in my ability to care and to confront. I care for injuries and I confront hostilities. I can be both capable and vulnerable."

"I am responsible for my thoughts, words, and acts. I am always responsible for my behavior. I am never to blame others."

Theologically, the assertive lifestyle recognizes that loveless power violates, powerless love abdicates, but power and love in balance create justice.[14]

Does the adoption of assertiveness as a life-style mean that if a pastor has all the correct skills for expressing anger, caring for oneself, and dealing directly with conflict, all church fights will be resolved peaceably? Of course not! And here is the bind for many pastors. They believe that if only they could do the right thing or say the right thing then peace would surely prevail.

Not all church conflicts end with reconciliation. The pastor who out of a wholesome self-esteem acts responsibly in the midst of conflict may well decide that it is necessary to confront certain persons or perhaps simply to terminate the pastoral relationship with the congregation. Such decisions are certainly difficult to make. Those choices can be particularly hard because it soon becomes evident that caring for self does not always lead to harmony between the pastor and the congregation. However, the likelihood for clarifying issues and achieving respect for one another is much greater when care for oneself is a primary value for all parties involved. Pastors who take care of themselves handle the stress of anger and conflict much better, and consistently report that they have greater personal resources available for their ministry.

CHAPTER 6

Seasons of Stress and Growth

Adulthood is not a plateau; rather, it is a dynamic and changing time for all of us. Growth is like a river; you can dam it up, slow it up, divert it, but you can't ever stop it. (Roger L. Gould)[1]

Men prefer to forget how many possibilities are open to them. (Walter Kaufmann)[2]

Stress in manageable amounts encourages and promotes vital growth. The natural course of a pastor's ministry will have in it many occasions for personal development through times of stress. The progressive stages of adult life offer the benefits of new perspectives so the maturing pastor can cope better with stress. Progress in the handling of stress can be facilitated especially through the caring support of one's colleagues, through trusting relationships with them. Also, numerous institutional structures, from the seminary to the various judicatory levels and beyond, provide a variety of resources to aid the pastor in managing and benefiting from the seasons of stress and growth that mark every stage of the pastor's life and ministry.

The Changing Seasons for Ministry

My friend leaned back and drew three quick puffs on his pipe. Then he pondered a few moments as his mind raced back over his twenty-five years in the ministry.

Mike could see that he had changed significantly in his approach to ministry since his ordination in the mid-1950s.

Mike's thoughts began to form words. "I can roll a lot better now with what happens. I hardly complain or blame people anymore. I am also less uptight now about giving a job to a layperson. It is not like me to run around to pick up the pieces or make sure the job gets done the way I want it done. If the layperson drops the ball or the project slips down the drain, it goes down the drain. I can live with that. But twenty-five years ago I would not have said that—or I would not have been telling the truth if I did say it."

My question for Mike: "Why do you think you could not have done that twenty-five years ago?"

Three more puffs on the pipe while Mike reflected on his response. "Early in the ministry I felt the weight of the responsibility much more heavily. I felt much more of a responsibility to take [on myself] all of the weight [of] the church's ministry."

My next question: "What do you think changed your mind between then and now?"

This time Mike answered promptly, without any reference to his pipe. "I found out that I could not do it. I realized somewhere that I could not carry all of the weight myself. There was also the realization that 99 percent of the results would be the same with an expenditure of less time and energy on my part. I was doing a lot of spinning my wheels. There was a desperation to fill every minute."

Lazily, slowly, the pipe was raised back to Mike's lips. Clearly, he was not spinning wheels this day.

Daniel J. Levinson has concluded from his research on the adult male life cycle that the equivalent of an "era" —twenty-five years—was separating Mike's relaxed view of ministry from his initial days of frenzied scrambling.[3] Indeed, in those twenty-five years, Mike had passed through several major periods in the pattern of adult development. In those periods Mike had struggled variously with his own self-concept, his view of his vocation, and his relationships with his wife and children. Those periods of adult development, whether Mike had realized it or not, had had a profound impact upon his evolving, changing outlook toward his ministry and his reactions to the pressures of his work.

Crisis stages for growth. Important information about periods of clergy stress through the different stages of adult life was offered through the study published in 1971 by the Ministry Studies Board. Among the findings of this study, two were quite significant. First, stress is a common experience that can occur at any time in a pastor's ministry. Secondly, there are periods when stress is likely to be more intense for a pastor. The time of greatest stress for many pastors is the first five years of their ministry. Periods of heavier stress recur from the eighth to the twelfth year, and again after approximately twenty years of ministry. Although each individual pastor may not experience this precise pattern, the statistical findings clearly suggest that there is a cyclical contour to job-related stress for clergy.[4]

James Glasse has suggested that through the development of the pastor's career there will be three predictable crises.[5] He specifically concurs with the Ministry Studies report that the first crisis will occur in the first three to five years of ministry. The crisis at this early stage of ministry, according to Glasse, occurs because the pastor (usually young) has the shock of making the transition from being a full-time student to becoming a full-time parish minister. Even fieldwork experiences in seminary, including an intern year, cannot protect the young pastor from this initial crisis. The question arises, "Is this the work I really want to do?" Probably by the fifth year the pastor has examined various vocational options and made a basic decision that resolves this crisis, the first professional turning point. The usual options the pastor has to consider, according to Glasse, include leaving the ministry, choosing another area of specialization in ministry, or continuing with essentially the same type of ministry begun after ordination.

The second crisis that Glasse identifies is the "point of no return," which occurs at about age forty. At this age pastors know what their place in ministry will be. From this point on there will be twenty or twenty-five more years of about the same type of work. Those who can enthusiastically affirm their present ministry will stay on for what will likely be a productive career. Others will say no and decide to find work outside the ordained ministry. Some will not make a clear, affirmative decision, but will just hang on and vent their inner dissatisfactions through the "conform/complaint syndrome."[6]

The third crisis discussed by Glasse is the time at age sixty or sixty-five when a pastor retires. This is frequently a crisis, because pastors are often not ready emotionally or financially for this transition. Now the pastor faces many of the same problems confronted on entering the ministry—only the problems are now in reverse as one begins to work one's way *out* of a full-time profession. The significance of this professional crisis can hardly be overstated, and many clergy ease the shock of this transition by responding to opportunities for part-time or interim pastoral positions.

Charles Stewart has identified five transition periods in a pastor's professional development, but all are not as closely related to age as Glasse's three crises seem to be.[7] Stewart concurs, however, with the *entrance* crisis for the young pastor out of seminary three to five years. This is when the young pastor is saying, "The ministry is not what I expected it to be." The next critical stage concerns how and whether one will make satisfactory *advancements.* The questions that haunt the pastor are, "How am I doing in comparison to seminary classmates? Am I being passed up by the church hierarchy?" Then the next stage is the *maintenance level,* when one is deciding "not to rock the boat." The questions that pass through the pastor's mind are: "Is there something I have yet to achieve, or should I continue doing what I am doing? Look how hard my younger colleagues are working. Should I join them, or claim time for relaxing? Certainly I have earned it."

The time of *decline* is the period when a pastor observes that some colleagues are retiring, dying, or moving to warmer climates. In quiet, reflective moments the pastor wonders, "Where are kindred spirits with whom I can share my concerns about the church? Why does preaching interest me less than it did ten years ago?" The *retirement* stage, of course, raises that profound question, "Is this all there is?" and "How can I retain self-respect among colleagues and friends if I am not working full time?"

The crisis that may lead to care of self. As pastors move through the natural stages of their ministry, there is evidence that many of them, both men and women, allow themselves to become obsessed with the drive for advancement, what Levinson calls the effort "to build a better life for oneself and to be affirmed by the tribe."[8] Translated into ecclesiastical language, it is the effort to establish oneself as a "rising star" in one's community, judicatory, or denomination. When this natural drive for advancement overwhelms the pastor's own personal identity, the pastor begins to conclude: "I am my success. I am my accomplishments. Therefore, if I do not make great accomplishments, I am nothing." That kind of reasoning leads to confusion of identity and loss of perspective on one's self, one's priorities, and one's ministry. The center of the pastor's life is the drive toward the illusion of success.

There are several ways to get through this crisis. (1) Have a heart attack. (2) Leave the ministry out of sheer exhaustion. (3) Have an affair so you have to leave the ministry. (4) Have a breakdown in your family relationships, something that may be indicated by the disruptive behavior of one of your children. (5) Recover full responsibility for self and regain a personal perspective that is not captive to every drive and urge toward success. In other words, reaffirm the strength of self that does not confuse personal self-esteem with one's achievements. Many have chosen this fifth option as the best way to care for themselves, and they tell how much they now enjoy their ministry.

Pastor Tim Grant, forty-one, can acknowledge now that he failed to become the messiah he had expected to be when he graduated from seminary. Indeed, after ordination he had worked with as much dedication and sincerity as any of his colleagues. He was duly rewarded with appointments to important committees in his judicatory. He was a man who incessantly needed people to like him. His motivators for ministry were guilt and anxiety. He did not go through a turbulent crisis, but he had his eyes opened when he served five years as an associate for a pastor who was a "real workaholic." Grant decided he would try not to emulate his mentor. Most notably, he has found "success" to be less satisfying than he had imagined. He reflects:

> I sit at some of those meetings, on boards that I looked at a couple years ago and said, "Gee, I wonder if I'll ever be able to get there, and if I do, will I do anything when I get there?" And now that I am there, I keep asking myself the question, "What the hell am I doing here? I really don't want to be here!" My standards now are that I can take care of myself without feeling guilty about it.

I can spend time with my wife and son without feeling guilty about it. I do not have to work all the time, and that is all right.

Another pastor, Neal Parker, recalls that he had been programmed to be a successful minister. Everyone knew that he had what it took to make the congregation he was serving into a "successful" congregation. He explained, "I was satisfying what I considered my role expectations for a growing and successful minister." His crisis came when he had been in the parish ministry for ten years. He was working eighty hours a week at that time. The crisis of reevaluation came upon him through four separate but related events. The church officers were not certain he was using his time well and wanted his hours evaluated. His family life was collapsing because he was completely out of touch with his children and his wife. He received a call to serve outside the pastoral ministry, and he went through the program of a church career development center. In order to recover his own selfhood, he had to adopt new values for his ministry. Interpersonal relationships took on new meaning instead of simply being used for achieving success.

> In order to take better care of myself I had to live in relationship with other people. I realized that relationships with others would be the springboard out of which the meaning of life would come for me. That meant that I needed for my own life a close relationship with my family, and personal relationships with the church members and officers, and also with my peers. I also realized that in cultivating those relationships and in sharing with those persons, I would have a meaningful personal life and a productive ministry.

Through the stages of adult life that all pastors face in fairly predictable order, the task of the self remains the same. The goal is not to avoid the crises of growth and development, but to maintain the perspective of spirit.

From that perspective the self retains the power of its own decision-making and avoids the helplessness of regarding itself as a victim of circumstances. The sequential periods of life and ministry are not a series of traps. They are more like different countries through which one travels. Always there are choices to be made; always there are forks in the road. The risk is to become preoccupied with some single aspect of the developmental journey. For many clergy the problem is that of being obsessed with the objective of establishing oneself as a successful pastor. But to make success the end toward which all else is sacrificed virtually guarantees that balance and perspective will be lost, integrity compromised, and relationships disrupted.

Taking responsibility for oneself and taking care of the vital areas of one's life and relationships is the primary task, no matter where one finds oneself in the adult developmental journey.

Meeting Stress Through Peer Relationships

Pastor George Tyler asked himself the important question, "What minister would I go to if I had a problem?"

Many clergy respond that there are no colleagues they would go to if they needed help. They find their colleagues pompous, or preoccupied with church budgets, status, or the numbers game. Others say that they do not find their professional peers to be good listeners. And some pastors admit that they are threatened by opportunities to be with their peers because they feel their own performance is being compared, and they feel that they come off second best.

The name for what often blocks clergy communication is "competition." Pastor Marcie Blake speaks directly to this matter.

I think our denominational structure is an isolating system because every pastor is basically in competition with
every other pastor. I find little trust among our pastors.
There is little sharing about their hurts, or about their
needs, or about their failures. I find pastors highly competitive. I am competitive myself. When my job depends
on how well I do in the congregation I am serving, and
your pulpit might be my next job, if I work it right—then
that just builds up immense barriers between us pastors.

Misunderstanding and mistrust keep many pastors
from finding in each other mutual support. However,
there is evidence that many pastors are finding supportive relationships with selected individuals and groups of
their colleagues as they risk sharing support and concern
for each other. One pastor described a Bible study group
in which he takes part with several other pastors. After
they discuss a Bible passage they use the remainder of
the time to talk about personal issues. It helps this pastor
to keep hold of a more realistic view of ministry. He
says, "It's helpful to refine my own idea of what ministry
is by talking with these guys." The self is strengthened
by such opportunities for balancing one's own views
against the viewpoints of colleagues.

Another pastor finds that his peer group helps ease the
stress and pressure of work so he does not dump all his
concerns on his wife. He explains: "Being in my support
group takes off the pressure that would otherwise be
created at home in the family situation. Then I do not
carry all the baggage home from the parish, and then I
do not have to use my wife as my only confidant. It takes
a load off her."

The pastoral peer group.   An increasing number of pastors are overcoming their professional mistrust and com-
petitiveness and offering one another support through a
pastoral peer group. If a pastor wishes to organize such
a group, these are factors to take into account:

1. *Who will be in the group?* Almost any two pastors could find something in common if they tried. A pastors' peer group, however, usually begins around a recognized common need. All the pastors may serve churches in the same area. They may all be seminary classmates. Or they may all be females with specific professional concerns. Some groups meet because "we all belong to the same denomination in our area, and we are known as the liberals." Other groups intend to be ecumenical so that pastors from a variety of traditions can meet one another.

Be careful about drawing the circle too tight. Do not assume that one Roman Catholic priest will feel out of place with seven Lutherans, or that one female pastor will not share the concerns of five males. One female pastor, in fact, after joining a pastors group in which she was the only woman, reported that she found it more supportive than the all-female group she was in earlier, which had dealt only with women's issues.

2. *What purpose does the group serve?* The peer group needs to have a specific purpose, and that purpose must match the felt needs of those in the group. When the purpose is not clear and only vaguely matches the needs of participants, enthusiasm for the group quickly wanes.

Clergy groups have many different purposes. Some groups meet to discuss "cases" that the members present out of their pastoral care work.[9] Other groups meet to discuss a book or to hear a member present a paper on a relevant subject. The purpose of a group may be simply to spend time together with no structured format, just to drink coffee and "rap." This last group meets for fellowship. Whatever the purpose may be, it is essential that it be understood and agreed upon by all. Otherwise, those who are confused about the purpose of the group will soon begin to absent themselves.

One way to create a group with a useful purpose is to

explore the various felt needs of those who want to be in a support group. Pastors usually express two important needs. One is to have an arena where they can get something off their chests that has them angry or upset. They want someone to listen to them. However, most pastors need a group that offers more than time for complaining. They want constructive support, suggestions, and appropriate confrontation that will enable them to grow and to function more effectively with greater skill as pastors.

Secondly, the personal element is essential to the purpose of the group. One pastor made that point about himself and his colleagues when he commented: "Ministers never seem to talk about what they are personally feeling with their peers. They talk about how other people are feeling about them or how successful their programs are. But they do not reveal themselves." Even a group that discusses systematic theology can do so in a manner that permits the expression of personal feelings. When there is sufficient freedom and trust for this personal element to occur, members will find the group more rewarding and will anticipate returning to subsequent meetings.

3. *What is our contract?*   A group cannot function without agreement regarding the time, frequency, and length of the meetings. There also needs to be agreement on a format for the meetings that will enable the group to accomplish its purpose.

Pastoral peer groups meet anywhere from once a week to once a month. Some meet for an hour, others spend an afternoon or a morning together. The common element for all such groups is that the set time is "sacred time," and only the most severe emergency can prevent a member from attending. The members of the group need to feel that their time together is a valuable commitment for all.

A group should consider a time-limited contract in which there is agreement to attend a certain number of meetings. At the end of the stated time, each member decides whether to continue longer with the group or not. When there is no agreement about the number of meetings and no contract for renegotiating at some definite date in the future, members will just drop out at will and the group will suffer a decline in morale as various members leave at different times.

Having a specific format helps a group to avoid the anxiety of creating its agenda anew each time it meets. Moreover, if there is no stated structure, different members may compete for the primary leadership role. Some form of agreed-upon order is necessary. In Glasse's outline for the case review, for example, the first five minutes are for giving information about the case. Then twenty-five minutes are used for analysis. Next, ten minutes are given to evaluate the presenting pastor's performance. The final ten minutes are for his or her reaction.[10] This type of structure ensures that the group will accomplish its task without unproductive wandering.

An essential element to any pastoral peer group is confidentiality. A peer group cannot function at all unless there is an explicit understanding that what is said and heard will be kept in strict confidence. This concern applies both to the participants and to information that may be shared in the group about parishioners or others outside the group. The best rule is that "everything discussed in the group stays in the group." This rule must be carefully observed. Even so, each group member will decide over a period of time how much to trust the group with personal feelings and information. Unless a group can establish more than a superficial level of trust, its helpfulness to its members will be limited.

Another element necessary to a peer support group is

the "buoyancy" factor.[11] This is a spirit conveyed by the group that anyone in it will not be allowed to "go under." That does not mean that group members can actually fight each other's battles. It does mean, however, that no group member is totally alone, unless that person chooses to be. If a member is willing to share a burden, the group guarantees understanding, appropriate confrontation, and most of all, support. With a support group like that in one's ministry, it is virtually impossible to go under. One pastor put it this way:

> There is nothing that I cannot share with my group and I know they will probe, challenge, support, and console. We take turns being friend and pastor to one another. We take one another to task when that needs to be done, too. You know that when you have a problem it will be dealt with. That is not frightening. That is supportive!

If a pastor tries to practice ministry as the "Lone Ranger" without emotional support from others, that pastor runs the risk of paying a high price. Sidney Jourard comments on the cost of avoiding the risk of being known by others.

> Every maladjusted person is a person who has not made himself known to another human being and in consequence does not know himself. Nor can he be himself. More than that, *he struggles actively to avoid becoming known by another human being.* He *works* at it ceaselessly, twenty-four hours daily, and it is work! In the effort to avoid becoming known, a person provides for himself a cancerous kind of stress which is subtle and unrecognized, but none the less effective in producing not only the assorted patterns of unhealthy personality which psychiatry talks about, but also the wide array of physical ills that have come to be recognized as the province of psychosomatic medicine.[12]

When a pastor intentionally creates a support network of persons with whom problems can be shared and joys celebrated, that pastor is in a much better position to keep the pressures of ministry well within manageable limits.

Institutional Support Structures for Ministry

The institutional church is the context for professional ministry. Although the form of the institutional church varies widely, most pastors function within a denominational organization that is not likely to change very soon. All such organizations are a strange mixture of high ideals and human folly. They provide both a helpful and a frustrating context in which to develop the professional ministry. That being the case, the fact remains that the individual pastor is the person with the most power for deciding how stress will be managed in ministry. However, the pastor need not stand alone. The institutional church has structures that offer vital supportive resources to the pastor. The decisions made at the judicatory and seminary levels as well as in other supportive agencies play a critical role in offering pastors a wider range of options for maximizing their self-care for the sake of ministry.

Judicatories. At both the national and the regional level, the major denominations have struggled for years with the personal and vocational problems faced by the parish pastor. Most regional governing bodies of the denominations have some means for providing pastors with vocational and personal counseling when they are clearly in need of it. However, some pastors think that judicatory leaders do not understand the stresses that exist at the parish level. Nonetheless, many judicatories have made a genuine effort to be supportive and helpful to the parish clergy.[13]

Rarely, however, does the parish pastor hear from judicatories that "taking care of oneself" is not only consistent with ministry, but a prerequisite to ministry.

Whether intended or not, the message many parish pastors hear from their judicatories is: "Work harder and longer hours to be a more effective pastor." All parish pastors are aware, usually even before ordination, that the system frequently rewards those who work hard and remain loyal, without regard for their own or their family's welfare. The rewards include upward mobility in the system and appointment to the more desirable churches. The impression given is that the system does not reward those who place a high priority upon taking care of themselves, and to the extent that this is true the system is defeating itself.

The time has come to reverse this trend so parish pastors may begin to hear a new message from their judicatory leaders. For example, regional-level judicatories should offer "Self-Care for Ministry" workshops. Within a two- or three-day retreat format, pastors should be challenged to examine their lives from a wholistic viewpoint, taking into account all of the stress areas of their ministry. This wholistic approach should be buttressed with a theological understanding that bases the stewardship of life upon a need for responsible self-care.

Stress in ministry is a much larger issue than the number of hours a person works each week. The chief issue is how to strengthen the whole person as a responsible self who needs care, and how to help judicatories encourage parish pastors to take better care of themselves for the sake of ministry.

Seminary education. The church's seminaries are faced with a difficult task. In three or four academic years, they are to prepare a person to function effectively as a pastor. That task is not just to train the seminarian intellectually, but to form the whole person—mind, spirit, and emotions.[14] These are ambitious goals for any institution of higher education, and theological seminaries do make remarkable strides toward achieving those important goals.

The fundamental irony of seminary education is that the candidate for ministry is prepared in an academic environment for a profession that is practiced essentially in a nonacademic setting. Certainly seminary educators are aware of this contradiction, and fieldwork programs and intern years help to introduce the seminarian to the nonacademic realm of the church, which the pastor will soon enter as a professional.

If the strenghtening of self through disciplined self-care were to be one of the chief priorities for a seminary education, two major issues would need to be addressed by a theological seminary. The first major issue is the nature of the seminarian's experience as a student. Because so much is supposed to be learned within three or four years, the seminary years for many students become very burdensome. Seminarians commonly report that they are coping at the limits of their personal, financial, and (in many instances) marital resources in order to complete an M.Div. program. Pastor Laura Clark reported that her seminary's academic catalog stated that the student should spend at least sixty hours per week doing coursework. When the dean was asked about that expectation, he explained, "That's the way it is in the parish, so you and your family can get used to it now in seminary." No wonder many new pastors have concluded that self-care and preserving one's marriage and one's personal wholeness are secondary to ministry.[15] Theological seminaries need to take a realistic view of what can be done with students in a three-year M.Div. program. Most of all, the seminary community can reinforce the insight that self-care is the basis for ministry, and make responsible self-care a primary value in that particular seminary community.

The second major issue that must be addressed by

theological seminaries is the dependent and passive role assumed by many ministerial students. For too many students, college and graduate school become a system for programmed passive-dependency. The program is outlined in the school's catalog, where all the courses and various requirements are spelled out for graduation. The catalog essentially outlines the hurdles that must be overcome, with designated procedures and allotted times for doing so. At the end of the obstacle course a reward is granted, with appropriate pageantry, on commencement day. That exercise marks the end of at least nineteen years (uninterrupted in many cases) of academic conditioning in which the student has learned well the art of leaping hurdles for certain rewards.

It is difficult for a student to pass through so many years of conditioning without becoming "passive-dependent." The rules of the game state simply that if you do what you are told to do, the institution predictably gives you what you need. Unfortunately, pastors then enter ministry with their well-learned passive-dependent behaviors. But the church is not waiting with catalogs telling one what to do, with obvious rewards for hours of hard work. Rather, the institutional church is waiting for pastors who have been prepared to think and function maturely on their own because they have a developed and strong sense of self. But mature selfhood based on initiative and responsibility will not be demonstrated in the parish unless a person has first learned the practice of self-care.

Most seminary educators are aware of the passive-dependent outlook that seminary education can encourage in students. If seminaries will consciously emphasize the high spiritual priority for self-care, a beginning step will be made in diminishing the dependency and the passivity that students learn from academic structures.

Continuing education. Opportunities for continuing

professional education are a vital resource enabling a parish pastor to develop personal wholeness. The wise pastor will work from a two- or three-year plan for continuing education that picks up the major areas where growth is needed. Unfortunately, too many pastors are influenced by the latest brochure that comes in the mail as they make plans for getting away from the parish for a few days. Mark Rouch identifies uncoordinated continuing education as a major problem for clergy.

> A major weakness in our continuing education has been that we have seen it as occasional, random participation in an educational episode. We read a book, enroll in a course, attend a seminar, and then say that we have done continuing education.
>
> > I stick in a thumb
> > And pull out a plum
> > And say, "What a good boy am I."[16]

The coordinated education plan that spans several years not only gives continuity to one's development but also demonstrates to the officers in one's church that forethought and stewardship have gone into the use of the resources which they make available for this purpose.

There are also resources available through the Society for the Advancement of Continuing Education for Ministry (855 Locust Street, Collegeville, Pa. 19426). The Society produces a "Continuing Education Resource Guide" that lists principal schools and agencies offering courses and workshops for clergy all across the country. For a small charge one can receive five Guides which will outline resources for every region of the country.

The pastor who is too busy to find enrichment through continuing education has chosen purposely to take the low road which leads to diminished professional effectiveness.

Career development counseling.   Under the national office of the Church Career Development Council (475 Riverside Drive, New York, N.Y. 10115) there now exists throughout the country a network of centers that are a major resource to religious professionals. These centers are self-governing, nonprofit agencies that have been organized specifically to be resources for clergy and those preparing for ministry. Through extensive vocational and personality testing and the guidance of professional counselors, career development counseling helps the pastor plan wisely for a ministry that draws upon all the pastor's resources while strengthening the pastor's self and wholeness.

Because of the normal growth changes they experience every five to eight years, many pastors benefit from returning to a career center that frequently in order to set new goals for their ministry and their personal growth. Most denominations and judicatories encourage the periodic use of the resources of career development counseling. They recognize that clergy who make informed plans for their future ministry cope more effectively with the normal stresses of ministry and personal development.

Clergy are encouraged to talk with their regional judicatory office to find out what resources are available for career development counseling. Below is the current listing of accredited career development centers.

Career and Personal Counseling Service
St. Andrews Presbyterian College
Laurinburg, N.C. 28352
(919) 276-3162

Career Development Center
Eckerd College
St. Petersburg, Fla. 33733
(813) 867-1166, Ext. 356

Career Development Center
of the Southeast
531 Kirk Road
Decatur, Ga. 30030
(404) 371-0336

Center for the Ministry
7804 Capwell Drive
Oakland, Calif. 94621
(415) 635-4246

Center for the Ministry and
New England Career Center
70 Chase Street
Newton Centre, Mass. 02159

Clergy Career Support Services
3501 Campbell
Kansas City, Mo. 64109
(816) 931-2516

Lancaster Career Development Center
561 College Avenue
Lancaster, Pa. 17603
(717) 397-7451

Midwest Career Development Service
2501 North Star Road
Suite 200
Columbus, Ohio 43221
(614) 486-0469

Midwest Career Development Service
1840 Westchester Boulevard
P.O. Box 249
Westchester, Ill. 60153
(312) 343-6268

North Central Career Development Center
3000 Fifth Street, N.W.
New Brighton, Minn. 55112
(612) 636-5120

Northeast Career Center
291 Witherspoon Street
Princeton, N.J. 08540
(609) 924-4814

Southwest Career Development Center
P.O. Box 5923
Arlington, Tex. 76011
(817) 265-5541

Accreditation Pending

Career and Personal Counseling Center
1904 Mt. Vernon Street
Waynesboro, Va. 22980
(703) 943-9997

Mid-South Career Development Center
P.O. Box 120815
Nashville, Tenn. 37212
(615) 327-9572

Programs in Canada

Contact:
Resources for Ministry
600 Jarvis Street
Toronto, Ont. M4Y2J6
(416) 924-9192

Counseling resources for clergy. Many pastors from time to time need the professional help of a counselor or psychotherapist. Making use of such resources is no longer viewed as a weakness by most pastors and judicatory leaders. Indeed, it is usually regarded as a mark of maturity to recognize the benefit that such help can be.

Competent professional resources are available to most clergy within a reasonable driving distance. Certainly a professional therapist will be chosen with care. A pastor may inquire from trusted friends whom they regard as a reliable therapist. Often staff persons at the judicatory level can make good suggestions if a pastor feels comfortable advising judicatory persons that resources for therapy are being sought. A pastor may also be helped in locating a competent therapist by writing to the following offices:

> The American Association of Pastoral Counselors sets standards for pastors who have become specialists in pastoral psychotherapy and counseling.

> The American Association of Pastoral Counselors
> 3000 Connecticut Avenue, N.W.
> Suite 300
> Washington, D.C. 20008   (202) 387-0031

> The American Association for Marriage and Family Therapy sets standards for therapists from a variety of disciplines who are trained in the special approaches necessary for helping marriages and families.

> The American Association for Marriage and Family Therapy
> 924 West 9th Street
> Upland, Calif. 91786   (714) 981-0888

This chapter has discussed resources available to pastors as they move through seasons of stress and growth. The stages of adult development reflect the changing perspectives from which one can view each period of one's ministry. Peer relationships offer a network of support and collegiality that can broaden greatly the basic underpinnings for one's ministry. Institutional resources of the church at many different levels provide significant help to clergy who recognize that managing stress is not a struggle that they need to wage alone. Important resources outside the structure of one's own denomination are also available. Though quite different in what they offer to a pastor, these various resources do have much in common. Most importantly, they bring new perspectives, fresh approaches, and realistic hope for pastors who want to manage stress effectively in their ministry.

CHAPTER 7

A Strategy for Specific Change

"Would you tell me, please, which way I ought to go from here?"

"That depends a good deal on where you want to get to," said the Cat.

"I don't much care where—" said Alice.

"Then it doesn't matter which way you go," said the Cat.

"—so long as I get *somewhere,*" Alice added as an explanation.

"Oh, you're sure to do that," said the Cat, "if you only walk long enough." (Lewis Carroll)[1]

If you don't know where you're going, you'll probably end up somewhere else. (David P. Campbell)[2]

Most of the readers of this book will not be helped simply because they have read it. Some may have found a few ideas interesting, even stimulating enough to underline, perhaps sufficiently noteworthy to mention to their spouse or to a friend. But for most readers it will be back to "business as usual," with no lessening of the stress in their ministry, because they will not follow through on the recommendations of this chapter. Many clergy are like the executives to whom Dr. Roy Menninger remarked:

Most of us live from day to day, so swamped by the pressures and details of daily life that we don't take the time to think about our goals in life. We're like the airplane pilot who radios the control tower and says, "Yeah, I'm lost, but I'm making great time."[3]

Those, however, who do want a new beginning toward reducing stress and finding greater satisfaction in their ministries and personal lives will now be given practical steps for doing so. This brief chapter may be the most important chapter of the book!

Assessing Areas for Change

Pastor Jim Larson decided that it was time for some changes in his ministry.[4] He knew that, at the rate he was going, his ministry would collapse in about three more years under the weight of all the stress he was carrying. Being somewhat organized, Larson devised a systematic plan for examining each area of his ministry and his personal life. He sat down in his office for an uninterrupted hour and a half. Specifically he asked himself how well he had been caring for himself. He tried to be honest with himself, and on a sheet of paper he made brief notations to indicate how much change was needed to diminish the stress level that was affecting his ministry. He simply put an "N" for "No change," an "S" for "Some change," and an "M" for "Much change." His self-evaluation followed the general pattern outlined below. Figure 1 illustrates his systematic notations.

Spiritual journey. "I had never thought, before, of my own spiritual life being so closely related to stress. I certainly have often breathed frantic prayers, 'Lord, grant me the serenity to survive this day,' but I have never thought of spirituality as a way to strengthen myself and gain a new perspective on handling stress. I need to take a serious look at my spirituality." (M)

Marriage. "I wonder if Mary really believes me when I tell her that our marriage means more to me than this church does? Why does she still have a faint look of disbelief in her eyes when I say how much she and the girls mean to me?" (S)

Interests. "How much of my time in this job is spent doing what I really enjoy? Certainly my creativity is welcomed by the congregation at least three quarters of the time. But I have not done any woodworking in my shop for nearly three years. Some change is needed there." (S)

Messiah. "No, I gave that one up several years ago. My church council knows very well after five years that I am quite human. I am going to keep it that way for my sake and for their sake." (N)

Untangling responsibility. "I wonder if I do too much blaming of others. Now as I think about it, when I feel depressed I am usually blaming Bill Hawkins and Pete Slade on the council for being so shortsighted about the mission of the church. Mary has said, too, that I am a bore to be around when I am singing the 'poor me' blues." (M)

Time. "I believe I handle time fairly well. But I wonder if my family knows what my schedule is from one week to the next. They probably think there is no planning for how I manage my time. If I had just five more hours a week, I would start exercising and lose those fifteen pounds that Doc Adams keeps mentioning." (S)

Anger/conflict. "More recently, I have had to risk conflict in our council meetings. I know my officers appreciate it when I tell them plainly what my views and feelings are. Right now I feel all right about how I am handling my anger within the church." (N)

Crisis stages. "I have begun to feel restless about this church. Why do I want to consider a call to another church? Is the congregation getting tired of me? Is this my last chance to be called to a good church? I need to talk with some of my friends to see if it's normal to feel this way at my age." (M)

Peer relationships. "I couldn't get along without my support group that meets every other week. I have good relationships with several pastors with whom I can discuss any aspect of my ministry. This area is solid for me." (N)

Support structures. "Here I need to do more intentional planning. I heard Tom and Chuck talk about their positive experiences at the career development center, but I have put off evaluating my own career. Along with that I have let my continuing education plans slide, too. I need to change here for certain!" (M)

Pastor Larson began to wonder what others might say to him about how he was dealing with stress. "Maybe I have been kidding myself in a few areas here," he thought out loud. "If I were really serious, I should get Mary's opinions and the views of at least two parishioners and a couple of my peers. If they agree with my own personal assessment, that would suggest that I have a pretty accurate view of myself. But I may have some blind spots where I don't want to be honest with myself."

It took Pastor Larson about four weeks to talk with his wife, two parishioners, and two colleagues from other churches.[5] His parishioners and colleagues were happy to have lunch with him and talk about his personal self-evaluation. When he had finished those five individual conversations, Larson completed for himself his *assessment profile.* He found that he had to leave some areas blank because not everyone could evaluate him in all ten areas. He also included a column for professional evaluation that he will complete when he goes through the program at a career development center.

Figure 1
ASSESSMENT PROFILE

	SELF	SPOUSE	PARISHIONER #1	PARISHIONER #2	PEER #1	PEER #2	PROFESSIONAL
Spiritual journey	M	S			N	S	
Marriage	S	S			N	S	
Interests	S	N			N	N	
Messiah	N	N	M	N	S	S	
Untangling responsibility	M	S	N	S	M	S	
Time	S	M	S	S	S	S	
Anger/conflict	N	N	N	N	N	N	
Crisis stages	M	S					
Peer relationships	N	N	N	N	N	N	
Support structures	M	S			S	N	

N = No change   S = Some change   M = Much change

Blank spaces indicate that the person had insufficient data on which to give me feedback.

Developing a Needs Profile

Pastor Larson quickly saw what the next step would be. He took a pad of paper and started listing the needed changes that his conversations had shown to be necessary if he were to have a greater sense of balance and wholeness in his personal life and his ministry. When he listed his "needs for change," he was aware that not everyone had agreed about how well he was handling stress in his ministry. Although he thought he had the messiah issue licked, his two peers and one of his parishioners were not nearly so certain. They saw him still trying to perform miracles in his ministry. He did not agree, but he decided to take their observations seriously.

Putting all those conversations together, Larson's "Needs Profile" began to take shape. See Figure 2.

Figure 2

NEEDS PROFILE

I need . . .

(1) to find a fresh approach to my devotional and spiritual life
(2) to be more sensitive to Mary so she will know how much I love her
(3) to spend more time in hobbies and leisure-time activities
(4) to look at my tendencies to play the messiah
(5) to stop blaming others
(6) to work out a better weekly schedule so my family will know when they can count on me being at home
(7) to understand better the career decisions facing me now
(8) to make plans to do career evaluation at a church career development center

Where Good Intentions Meet the Test

Everything Pastor Larson did up to this point would have been a waste of time if he had stopped here. He had developed quite reliable data for assessing his effectiveness in managing stress, but that did not change anything. He would have gone right back to the same stressful routine if he did nothing more with his good intentions. If stress was in fact to become more manageable, and if his ministry was to benefit because of it, two more steps were absolutely necessary. Pastor Larson had to set concrete goals, and he had to "go public" with his strategy for change.

Actually, the second parishioner Pastor Larson talked to advised him about how to set goals for change. He told Larson to follow these four steps if he really intended to make changes for the better.

a. Begin the statement of all your goals with the words *"I will . . ."* Do not use the phrase "I will try . . ." Intention, no matter how good, without commitment never changed anything, and certainly not a pastor!

b. *Be realistic.* If your goals are unattainable, you are setting yourself up for certain failure and more discouragement. Setting goals for dealing with stress is not like dreaming up New Year's resolutions! Choose goals that stretch you, that involve some risk and growth, but be certain they can be achieved. Part of being realistic is not to adopt too many goals. Five to ten goals for the next three years are enough.

c. *Be specific.* Avoid generalities that sound wonderful. This rule especially helped Larson as he considered his marriage. He was tempted to write down as a goal, "I will be more thoughtful of Mary's feelings." But then he realized the necessity for being specific and concrete, so he wrote instead, "I will ask Mary to go out to eat with me without the kids once a month."

    d. *Use time deadlines.* This is one way to hold yourself accountable. Unless we commit ourselves to reach a goal by a specific time, we probably are not serious about the goal in the first place. It may feel good to have a particular goal, but without a time deadline to prod us, we are not likely to achieve the goal.

Pastor Larson had at first been skeptical about goal-setting. He had always been dubious about borrowing models from secular industry and trying to apply them to the work of the church. But at the urging of his parishioner, whom he respected, he looked at his Needs Profile to see what possible specific goals could emerge. He sat down again in his study with paper and pencil. After another hour and a half, Larson had developed a sound strategy, tailored to his needs. It was a plan for bringing the stress in his ministry and in his personal life under much better control. See Figure 3.

Finally, Pastor Larson took one last step, which he knew had to come if he were to be faithful to his intentions to make changes. *He went public with his strategy for change.* He took an evening to share his plans with his wife, and gave her a copy of his goals. She was pleased with some of the goals he had adopted. She was skeptical as to whether he would follow through on other goals. But she assured him of her support for his effort to manage his stress better and to improve their home life.

Figure 3

GOAL SETTING:
STRATEGY FOR MANAGING STRESS

I will . . .

(1) within four months have a two-year continuing education plan for attending workshops and courses on spirituality

(2) ask Mary to go out to eat with me without the kids once a month

(3) work one evening a week in my woodworking shop

(4) review with the pastor-parish relations committee, over the next 4 months, those areas where my parishioner and 2 peers say I have messiah tendencies

(5) immediately stop blaming others for my frustrations, and join a racquetball club within three weeks so I will have ways for releasing my anger energy

(6) plan my weekly schedule each Sunday afternoon and post it on the refrigerator door so my family will know when I will be home

(7) at the next meeting of my support group bring up my concerns about the effectiveness of my ministry

(8) go to a career development center within one year

Next, Pastor Larson went to lunch with the president of the church council. With a copy of his strategy in hand, they went over each of his goals. They agreed to have lunch together again in about four months, when Larson would report how well he was adhering to his strategy. He also knew that he needed to tell his support group about his strategy for change and coping with stress. The group, upon hearing his plans, agreed to encourage his efforts, and asked him to update them periodically about his progress toward the goals.

If Pastor Larson had not chosen to *go public* and to share his plans with several people, he would have been playing it safe by allowing himself the option of making no changes in his work style and life-style. His plans most likely would have remained only good intentions, and he would have continued to feel overwhelmed by the stress in his ministry.

Mark Rouch has made two important observations that point up the basic issues in managing stress for ministry. First, a career is like floating down a river on a raft. If the raft is rudderless, it will be captive to the current, going wherever the river takes it, needing only a push now and then away from the shore. The pressures, currents, and stresses manage the raft, which is essentially at the mercy of the river. Thus, to drift aimlessly with the flow of life is not to manage stress. Rouch has a second observation: "To become intentional is, essentially, to take charge of one's own life, to be inner-directed rather than other-directed, . . . to choose career goals and work toward them."[6]

Rouch's wisdom reflects the insight of an earlier pastor who urged his colleagues not to be conformed to this world (Rom. 12:2). When stress manages the minister, the minister is the victim of conformity to this stressful age. And for most pastors, unless the steps outlined in this chapter are followed and a strategy for stress management is mapped out, stress will continue to be the manager instead of the pastor managing stress. But ministry that is based upon conscious attention to one's own needs and relationships will have the greater resources for many years of lively and rewarding service to God and neighbor.

Notes

Chapter 1
THE DIMENSIONS OF STRESS IN MINISTRY

1. Robert D. Phillips and Thomas H. McDill, "The Mental Health of Presbyterian Ministers and Their Families: A Study by the Permanent Committee on Christianity and Health" (General Assembly, Presbyterian Church U.S., 1966), p. 2.

2. Jerry Edelwich with Archie Brodsky, *Burn-Out: Stages of Disillusionment in the Helping Professions* (Human Sciences Press, 1980), p. 14.

3. Ibid.

4. Hans Selye, *The Stress of Life,* rev. ed. (McGraw-Hill Book Co., 1976), p. 1.

5. Phillips and McDill, p. 3.

6. Selye, *The Stress of Life,* rev. ed., p. 74.

7. Hans Selye, *The Stress of Life* (McGraw-Hill Book Co., 1956), p. 299.

8. Herbert J. Freudenberger, "The Staff Burn-Out Syndrome in Alternative Institutions," *Psychotherapy: Theory, Research and Practice,* Vol. 12, No. 1 (Spring 1975), p. 73. See also Herbert J. Freudenberger, "Burn-Out: Occupational Hazard of the Child Care Worker," *Child Care Quarterly,* Vol. 6, No. 2 (Summer 1977), pp. 90–99.

9. Clarence L. Barnhart and Robert K. Barnhart (eds.), *The World Book Dictionary,* Vol. 1 (Field Enterprises Educational Corp., 1977), p. 267.

10. "Teacher Burnout," *Instructor,* Vol. 88, No. 6 (Jan. 1979), p. 57.

11. Ibid. Note that the presence of these various symptoms may indicate mental or emotional problems other than burnout.

12. Edelwich and Brodsky, *Burn-Out,* pp. 28–29.

13. Richard C. W. Hall, Earl R. Gardner, Mark Perl, Sondra K. Stickney, and Betty Pfefferbaum, "The Professional Burnout Syndrome," *Psychiatric Opinion,* Vol. 16, No. 4 (April 1979), pp. 12–17. See also Tobias Brocher, "Coping with Stress," *Resource,* Vol. 4, No. 4 (Sept./Oct. 1979), p. 2. Brocher describes four areas in which our bodies signal that we are under too much stress. The first area is that of cardiovascular symptoms such as heart rate acceleration and high blood pressure. The second area includes gastrointestinal symptoms such as heartburn and ulcers. The third area relates to respiratory illnesses such as the common cold, which can indicate that one is under excessive stress. The fourth area includes certain types of asthma, rashes, or eczema, which can be caused by stress. A similar list of symptoms for recognizing signs of stress is outlined by psychiatrists Barrie S. Greiff and Preston K. Munter in their book entitled *Tradeoffs: Executive, Family, and Organizational Life* (New American Library, 1980), p. 159.

14. Edgar W. Mills and John P. Koval, *Stress in the Ministry* (Washington, D.C.: Ministry Studies Board, 1971). On page 2 the authors refer to a three-level model for understanding the progress of career-related stress that leads to the person leaving the ministry. See also Charles William Stewart, *Person and Profession: Career Development in the Ministry* (Abingdon Press, 1974). On pages 17–18 Stewart refers to studies showing that instead of breaking down under career stress, clergy are choosing to leave the ministry.

15. Seward Hiltner, *Ferment in the Ministry* (Abingdon Press, 1969), p. 19.

16. Mills and Koval, *Stress in the Ministry,* pp. 57–58. Four fifths of the nearly 15,000 pastors in their study reported a satisfactory resolution of their difficulties.

17. Donald C. Houts, "Pastoral Care for Pastors: Toward a Church Strategy," *Pastoral Psychology,* Vol. 25, No. 3 (Spring 1977), p. 189.

18. Ibid., p. 190.

19. G. Lloyd Rediger, "Clergy Burnout," *Church Management,* Vol. 56, No. 8 (July 1980), p. 10.

20. Margaretta K. Bowers, *Conflicts of the Clergy: A Psychodynamic Study with Case Histories* (Thomas Nelson & Sons, 1963), pp. 9–10, 232.

21. Urban T. Holmes III, *The Future Shape of Ministry: A Theological Projection* (Seabury Press, 1971), p. 150.

22. Donald P. Smith, *Clergy in the Cross Fire: Coping with Role Conflicts in the Ministry* (Westminster Press, 1973). "Role conflict occurs when two or more role expectations interfere with each other or contradict one another altogether" (p. 26). "When the expectations of others are unclear or confusing, the focal person experiences role ambiguity" (p. 27).

23. Mills and Koval, *Stress in the Ministry,* p. 4.

24. Clifford J. Sager (*Marriage Contracts and Couple Therapy: Hidden Forces in Intimate Relationships;* Brunner/Mazel, 1976) writes: "Unwritten marriage contracts contain clauses that cover most aspects of feelings, needs, activities, and relationships. Some of the clauses are known to the contract maker, others are beyond awareness" (p. 9).

25. See Irene Lovett, "Pastor on a Pedestal," in Thomas E. Kadel (ed.), *Growth in Ministry* (Fortress Press, 1980), pp. 81–93.

26. Milo L. Brekke, Merton P. Strommen, and Dorothy L. Williams, *Ten Faces of Ministry* (Augsburg Publishing House, 1979), p. 9.

27. See William E. Hulme, *Your Pastor's Problems* (Doubleday & Co., Inc., 1966), Ch. 3, "The Need to Succeed," pp. 47–59.

28. Mills and Koval, *Stress in the Ministry,* pp. 9–24, 54. Clergy will do well to note the observations of psychiatrists Greiff and Munter regarding the assumptions of young executives who climb toward success with the organization first, themselves second, and their families last in their priorities. Such priorities are based on these assumptions:

—that as the executive charges forward, the family will either remain static or develop according to his wishes and expectations

—that he will be able voluntarily to limit and modify a career pattern established over many years, during which his family has accepted second place in his life, and that he will eventually be able to give them first priority, picking up where he left off as though the years of deprivation did not count

—that the rewards of work will justify the neglect of self and family

—that the company will respect and reward him more for his zealous dedication and devotion

—that he can function optimally over a long period of time, sustaining himself with only minimal personal satisfaction.

Greiff and Munter declare, "Such ideas are not only naive but dangerous" (*Tradeoffs*, p. 15).

29. John C. Harris has defined judicatory as "a term used to describe any official regional association of congregations with a salaried executive leadership, e.g., a presbytery, an archdiocese, a diocese, a conference, an association." "New Trends in Pastoral Care for Pastors," *Pastoral Psychology*, Vol. 22, No. 212 (March 1971), p. 7.

30. Nancy Jo von Lackum and John P. von Lackum III, *Clergy Couples* (National Council of Churches, 1979), pp. 3–4.

31. This point is emphasized by Donald Smith: "Because there are complex causes [for role conflict and ambiguity], the solutions must involve the understanding and efforts not only of the clergy and of local congregations but of every part of the occupational system to which they belong. . . . Thus, in dealing with the incompatible expectations that impinge on the clergy, we must consider change in several different subsystems of the church at the same time if we are to effect a meaningful resolution of their problems " (*Clergy in the Cross Fire*, p. 115). See Smith's Ch. 8 for his full discussion.

Chapter 2
RECOVERING SELF FOR MINISTRY

1. Paul Tillich, *Systematic Theology*, Vol. I (University of Chicago Press, 1951), pp. 169–170.

2. David Baily Harned, *Faith and Virtue* (United Church Press, 1973), p. 48; cited in James B. Nelson, *Embodiment: An*

Approach to Sexuality and Christian Theology (Augsburg Publishing House, 1978), p. 115.

3. "A Service for Ordination and Installation," *The Worshipbook—Services and Hymns* (Westminster Press, 1972), p. 90. See also Mark 10:43–45.

4. Harry G. Goodykoontz, *The Minister in the Reformed Tradition* (John Knox Press, 1963), pp. 18–19.

5. James D. Smart, *The Rebirth of Ministry* (Westminster Press, 1960, repr. 1978), p. 28.

6. Daniel Jenkins, *The Gift of Ministry* (London: Faber & Faber, 1947), p. 20.

7. H. Richard Niebuhr and Daniel Day Williams (eds.), *The Ministry in Historical Perspectives* (Harper & Brothers, 1956), p. 1.

8. "Amazing Grace!" *The Worshipbook,* p. 296.

9. "Holy Spirit, Truth Divine," ibid., p. 422.

10. Jenkins, *The Gift of Ministry,* p. 19. Robert S. Paul (*Ministry;* Wm. B. Eerdmans Publishing Co., 1965) has spoken similarly of ministry: "Its essence is hidden in the One who, although he possessed the divine nature from the beginning, yet 'did not think to snatch at equality with God, but made himself nothing, assuming the nature of a slave.' This is the ministry which defines the nature of all Ministry, to which we must always return" (p. 239). "It can only be leadership in what it means to 'put yourself last,' for that is the only kind of leadership that is recognized in the Kingdom of God" (p. 189).

11. Henri J. M. Nouwen, *Creative Ministry* (Doubleday & Co., 1971), p. 111.

12. Goodykoontz, *The Minister in the Reformed Tradition,* p. 107.

13. John B. Cobb, Jr., *Theology and Pastoral Care* (Fortress Press, 1977), p. 12.

14. Ibid.

15. Ibid., p. 23.

16. Roberto Assagioli, *Psychosynthesis* (Viking Press, 1965), pp. 118–119.

17. Ibid., p. 119.

18. Cobb, *Theology and Pastoral Care,* pp. 25–42.

19. Ibid., p. 27.

20. John E. Biersdorf, "A New Model of Ministry," in John

E. Biersdorf (ed.), *Creating an Intentional Ministry* (Abingdon Press, 1976), p. 24.

21. Ibid., p. 23.

22. Paul Scherer, *For We Have This Treasure* (Harper & Brothers, 1944), pp. 38–39.

23. See Wayne E. Oates (ed.), *The Minister's Own Mental Health* (Channel Press, 1961).

24. Goodykoontz, *The Minister in the Reformed Tradition,* p. 19.

25. Ibid., p. 145.

26. Brekke et al., *Ten Faces of Ministry.*

27. Ibid., pp. 55–56.

28. Ibid., p. 56.

29. John C. Harris, *Stress, Power and Ministry* (Washington, D.C.: Alban Institute, 1977), p. 70.

30. Ibid.

31. Ibid., p. 71.

32. Nouwen, *Creative Ministry,* p. 51.

33. Ibid.

34. Robert G. Kemper, "Small Issues and Massive Revelation," in Biersdorf (ed.), *Creating an Intentional Ministry,* p. 171.

35. Tillich, *Systematic Theology,* Vol. II (1957), p. 61.

36. James B. Ashbrook, "Discussion of Hadden Paper," *Ministry Studies,* Vol. 2, Nos. 3, 4 (Oct. and Dec. 1968), pp. 30–36, cited in Smith, *Clergy in the Cross Fire,* pp. 86–87.

37. Brocher, "Coping with Stress," p. 5.

Chapter 3
PERSONAL RESOURCES FOR MANAGING STRESS

1. Nelson, *Embodiment,* p. 115.

2. Quoted with the permission of Henri J. M. Nouwen from "Solitude," a lecture given by him at the seventeenth annual convention of the American Association of Pastoral Counselors, Denver, Colo., April 11, 1980.

3. Retreat at the Jesuit Seminary at Wernersville, Pa., 1976.

4. Erik H. Erikson, *Identity: Youth and Crisis* (W. W. Norton & Co., 1968), pp. 96–107.

5. *Augustine: Confessions and Enchiridion,* ed. and tr. by Albert

C. Outler, Vol. VII of The Library of Christian Classics (Westminster Press, 1955), p. 31.

6. Matthew Fox, "Spirituality for Protestants," *The Christian Century,* Vol. 95, No. 25 (Aug. 1978), p. 736.

7. Brekke et al., *Ten Faces of Ministry,* pp. 56–57.

8. Ibid., p. 56.

9. Ibid.

10. William J. Lederer and Don D. Jackson, *The Mirages of Marriage* (W. W. Norton & Co., 1968), p. 199.

11. Readers can be aided in assessing their own marriage by referring to David R. Mace and Vera C. Mace, *What's Happening to Clergy Marriages?* (Abingdon Press, 1980). Chs. 3 and 4 discuss the principal issues that concern clergy and spouses about their marriages.

12. Lederer and Jackson, *The Mirages of Marriage,* pp. 364–369.

13. See ibid., p. 42, where reference is made to Harry Stack Sullivan, *Conceptions of Modern Psychiatry* (W. W. Norton & Co., 1953), pp. 42–43.

14. Gaylord Noyce, "The Tensions of Our Calling," *The Christian Ministry,* Vol. 11, No. 5 (Sept. 1980), p. 21.

15. Strong-Campbell Interest Inventory of the Strong Vocational Interest Blank, Revised 1981 (Stanford University Press, 1981).

16. Richard Nelson Bolles, *What Color Is Your Parachute? A Practical Manual for Job Hunters and Career Changers,* rev. ed. (Ten Speed Press, 1979), p. 173.

17. David D. Burns, "The Perfectionist's Script for Self-Defeat," *Psychology Today,* Vol. 14, No. 6 (Nov. 1980), p. 46.

18. Martin Buber, *Hasidism and Modern Man,* ed. and tr. by Maurice Friedman (Horizon Press, 1958), pp. 139–140; cited by Clark E. Moustakas, *Creativity and Conformity* (D. Van Nostrand Co., 1967), p. 27.

19. James D. Glasse, *Putting It Together in the Parish* (Abingdon Press, 1972), pp. 55–56.

20. Richard N. Bolles, *The Three Boxes of Life: And How to Get Out of Them* (Ten Speed Press, 1978), p. 382.

Chapter 4
MINISTRY WITHIN LIMITS

1. Wayne E. Oates, *Confessions of a Workaholic: The Facts About Work Addiction* (Abingdon Press, 1971), p. 12.

2. *Calvin: Institutes of the Christian Religion,* ed. by John T. McNeill and tr. by Ford Lewis Battles, Vol. XX of The Library of Christian Classics (Westminster Press, 1960), p. 773.

3. Ernest Becker, *The Denial of Death* (Free Press, 1973), p. 5.

4. Ibid., p. 26.

5. Richard Bach, *Illusions: The Adventures of a Reluctant Messiah* (Delacorte Press, 1977), pp. 40–42.

6. Glasse, *Putting It Together in the Parish,* pp. 19–20, 69–70.

7. John B. Cobb, Jr., *The Structure of Christian Existence* (Westminster Press, 1967), p. 121.

Chapter 5
COPING WITH TIME, ANGER, AND CONFLICT

1. "Our God, Our Help in Ages Past," *The Worshipbook,* p. 549.

2. The magnitude of the time problem for pastors is illustrated by the *Pastoral Activities Index* prepared for Presbyterian clergy. This manual shows no fewer than 192 professional activities divided among 8 major roles for the parish pastor! (The Vocation Agency, The United Presbyterian Church U.S.A., 1976).

3. Certainly the institution of the sabbath had its roots in an agricultural setting. See J. Morgenstern, "Sabbath," *The Interpreter's Dictionary of the Bible,* ed. by George Arthur Buttrick, Vol. 4 (Abingdon Press, 1962), pp. 135–141.

4. Merrill E. Douglass and Joyce McNally, "How Ministers Use Time," *The Christian Ministry,* Vol. 11, No. 1 (Jan. 1980), p. 23.

5. Ibid., pp. 23–24.

6. David Gasperson, "Inspecting the Minister: Can the

Minister Be Held Accountable?" *The Christian Ministry,* Vol. 11, No. 4 (July 1980), p. 31.

7. See John Wiens's outline for helping pastors and lay leaders to look together at the issue of time management for ministry: "The Annual Review of the Pastor-Church Relationship," *The Christian Ministry,* Vol. 6, No. 1 (Jan. 1975), pp. 10–13. See also Speed B. Leas, *Time Management: A Working Guide for Church Leaders* (Abingdon Press, 1978), particularly Ch. 3, "Role Conflict." Leas emphasizes the importance of the pastor being clear about how time is to be used: "If you let others take the initiative, you are quite likely to end up with a list of recommended activities that are not particularly interesting to you. If this is the case, it is guaranteed that you will procrastinate, become bored, and not put much energy into your profession. Excitement and energy come from those who do what they want to do and are convinced that what they are doing fits their personality best" (p. 75).

8. It is not intended here to suggest thirteen modules as a standard for parish ministry. Each pastor needs to determine what is the appropriate balance between work and personal time.

9. G. Lloyd Rediger, "Time Urgency," *Church Management,* Vol. 56, No. 6 (April 1980), p. 10.

10. Alan C. Filley, *Interpersonal Conflict Resolution* (Scott, Foresman & Co., 1975), p. 4.

11. Hiltner, *Ferment in the Ministry,* p. 45.

12. See John L. Hoff, "Conflict Management: An Organizational Principle," *The Christian Ministry,* Vol. 4, No. 1 (Jan. 1973), pp. 16–19. See also Eileen F. N. Guthrie and Warren Sam Miller, *Making Change: A Guide to Effectiveness in Groups* (Minneapolis: Interpersonal Communication Programs, 1978), Ch. 9, "The Role of Conflict: Using Tension Creatively."

13. Speed Leas and Paul Kittlaus, *Church Fights: Managing Conflict in the Local Church* (Westminster Press, 1973), pp. 132–134.

14. David W. Augsburger, *Anger and Assertiveness in Pastoral Care* (Fortress Press, 1979), p. 44. Note here Augsburger's reference to Paul Tillich, *Love, Power, and Justice* (Oxford University Press, 1954), pp. 39–40.

Chapter 6
SEASONS OF STRESS AND GROWTH

1. Roger L. Gould, *Transformations: Growth and Change in Adult Life* (Simon & Schuster, 1978), pp. 14, 322.

2. Walter Kaufmann, "I and You: A Prologue," in Kaufmann's translation of Martin Buber, *I and Thou* (Charles Scribner's Sons, 1970), p. 9.

3. Daniel J. Levinson et al., *The Seasons of a Man's Life* (Ballantine Books, 1979); see Ch. 2, "Eras: The Anatomy of the Life Cycle."

4. Mills and Koval, *Stress in the Ministry,* pp. 11, 13, 54.

5. Glasse, *Putting It Together in the Parish,* pp. 40–42.

6. Ibid., p. 41.

7. Stewart, *Person and Profession,* pp. 75–79.

8. Levinson et al., *The Seasons of a Man's Life,* p. 59.

9. Glasse, *Putting It Together in the Parish,* Chs. 7 and 8. In these chapters, Glasse outlines a case method of small-group study for pastors.

10. Ibid., pp. 88–91.

11. I first heard this descriptive term, the "buoyancy" factor, used by G. Lloyd Rediger.

12. Sidney M. Jourard, *The Transparent Self,* rev. ed. (Van Nostrand-Reinhold Co., 1971), pp. 32–33.

13. Speed Leas has explained that role conflicts prevent many denominational executives from being as supportive to their parish pastors as they would like to be. Denominational executives must balance the roles of pastor, supervisor, deployment officer, and consultant. Speed Leas, *A Study of Involuntary Terminations in Some Presbyterian, Episcopal, and United Church of Christ Congregations* (Washington, D.C.: Alban Institute, 1980), pp. 34–35.

14. See James I. McCord's discussion of the goals of theological education: "The Understanding of Purpose in a Seminary Closely Related to the Church," *Theological Education,* Vol. 14, No. 2 (Spring 1978), pp. 59–66.

15. For a discussion of self-care for seminarians see Charles L. Rassieur, "How Will Stress Affect Your Ministry?" *Seminary*

Quarterly, Vol. 22, No. 1 (Fall 1980), pp. 1–2.

16. Mark A. Rouch, *Competent Ministry: A Guide to Effective Continuing Education* (Abingdon Press, 1974), p. 21. See also articles by Connolly C. Gamble, Jr., David R. Jones, Paul Dietterich, Thomas E. Brown, and James L. Lowery, Jr., in *The Christian Ministry,* Vol. 5, No. 3 (May 1974), and articles by Connolly C. Gamble, Jr., David C. Pohl, Robert A. Raines, and George St. Angelo in *The Christian Ministry,* Vol. 9, No. 1 (Jan. 1978).

Chapter 7
A STRATEGY FOR SPECIFIC CHANGE

1. Lewis Carroll, *Alice's Adventures in Wonderland* (St. Martin's Press, 1977), p. 95.

2. David P. Campbell, *If You Don't Know Where You're Going, You'll Probably End Up Somewhere Else* (Niles, Ill.: Argus Communications, 1974).

3. Roy Menninger, as quoted by Berkeley Rice in "Midlife Encounters," *Psychology Today,* Vol. 12, No. 11 (April 1979), p. 95.

4. Pastor Larson is a fictional representative of the many pastors with whom I have worked who have used goal-setting to reduce stress in their ministries.

5. Not all pastors are married. If a pastor is single, someone who is well acquainted with his or her personal habits and work patterns should be consulted.

6. Rouch, *Competent Ministry,* pp. 138–139.